NETWORKING FOR NOVICES

by Susan Shelly

LearningExpress • New York

Shelly, Susan.
     Networking for novices/Susan Shelly.
          p.   cm.—(Basics made easy)
     ISBN 1–57685–143–5
     1. Job hunting. 2. Social networks. I. Title II. Series.
HF5382.7.S48   1998
650.14—dc21   98–65390
                                                                                  CIP

Printed in the United States of America
9 8 7 6 5 4 3 2 1
First Edition

Regarding the Information in this Book
Every effort has been made to ensure accuracy of directory information up until press time. However, phone numbers and/or addresses are subject to change. Please contact the respective organizations for the most recent information.

For Further Information
For information on LearningExpress, other LearningExpress products, or bulk sales, please call or write to us at:
     LearningExpress®
     900 Broadway
     Suite 604
     New York, NY 10003
     212-995-2566

LearningExpress is an affiliated company of Random House, Inc.

ISBN 1–57685–143–5

7 85555 85143 6

CONTENTS

CHAPTER | 1

GETTING
STARTED

If you're looking for a job, you're in good company. More than five million people are job hunting at any given time in this country. Don't worry, though! These statistics include prospective workers in every field from fast food to nuclear physics; you won't be competing with all of them.

You will be competing, however, and that's why you picked up this book. You want an advantage—something to give you an edge on the other job hunters out there. Well, you've come to the right place. In just 20 chapters, you'll learn how to establish and use a network, and having a network makes job hunting a much less daunting prospect.

In Chapter 3, you will learn in more detail what a network is. For now, very simply, let's just say that it's *the people that you know* and *the people that those people know*. It's also important to know what a network can do for you: A good network will not only make your job hunt easier; it also can enrich your personal life.

Through this book I will teach you, step by step, how to establish and maintain a network. If you're a good student, your network will last a lifetime. It will make job searches more efficient, less stressful, and more rewarding, and you will find ways to tap into your network for reasons that aren't job related, too.

WHAT CAN NETWORKING DO FOR ME?

Networking is used in many ways, often without even being recognized. Savvy people use networking for everything from locating good used cars to finding the best schools for their kids. Nowhere, though, is networking used more—or more effectively—than in job hunting and career advancement.

A good network will boost your chances for a successful job hunt immeasurably. A little help from your friends (and other contacts in your network) never hurts. Still, before we cover the basic information concerning résumés, interviews, and classified ads—all of which have direct ties to networking—you need to determine what job you want.

Take this simple true-or-false quiz to start. Don't get nervous; you'll do just fine. There are no "right" or "wrong" answers; the purpose of this exercise is to assess your readiness to start job hunting and show you which areas you need to concentrate on.

So, first things first. Take the quiz, then prepare to learn everything you'll need to know about networking. You can expect your job search—and your life!—to get a little bit easier.

IT'S QUIZ TIME!

1. I know exactly what kind of job I want. True / False
2. I have researched job trends and the projected job market to make sure the field I'm pursuing will put me in an employable position for the future. True / False
3. The help-wanted section of the classified ads is the best place to look for a job. True / False
4. I have a professional-quality résumé ready to use during my job search. True / False
5. I have a good cover letter ready that I can customize to use with my résumé. True / False

6. I know several well-qualified people who have agreed to give me references as needed during my job search. True / False

7. I have prepared for job interviews by reading, getting an idea of what questions are commonly asked, and preparing answers to those questions. True / False

8. I have a good understanding of interview etiquette, including the importance of timeliness, how to dress, what to say, and what not to say. True / False

9. Once I have an interview, I can sit back and wait for the phone to ring. True / False

10. I should take the first job I'm offered just because I need the experience. True / False

Didn't I tell you that would be easy? Let's see how you did.

If you answered "True" to questions 1, 2, 4, 5, 6, 7, and 8 and "False" to questions 3, 9, and 10, then you've obviously started preparing for your job hunt. If you answered "False" to any of questions 1, 2, 4, 5, 6, 7, or 8, then you've got your work cut out for you, but that's okay. Let's get started, together.

IDENTIFYING THE JOB YOU WANT

There are thousands of different jobs available out there, and you have to pick one that you want to pursue. Even though the one-career-per-person days are behind us (it's estimated that the average worker now has about 11 jobs and 3 careers over his or her working life), it's still important to choose a job (and a career) that will be rewarding, both personally and financially.

Let's take a look at some predictions for job trends and ways to identify jobs that might suit you.

Job? What Job?

You're looking for a job, but which job should you be looking for? This rapidly changing world gives us rapidly changing job opportunities. Check out a professional journal or even the classified ads of a big-city newspaper sometime. There are likely to be ads for jobs you have never heard of, much less have any interest in.

Experts at the U.S. Bureau of Labor and Statistics who study the changing face of employment have identified several areas of rapid growth. They have identified the following six fastest growing job areas as we move toward the 21st century:

- **Health care.** The United States soon will have 76 million baby boomers in their 50s. Needless to say, this large older population will lead to great increases in demand for health care and related industries.
- **Robotics.** Robots might still seem futuristic, but those who know about such things predict that we'll use far more of them as we enter the next century. They'll be much more sophisticated than the ones in use today. Robotics engineers, installers, technicians, and repair people will be needed.
- **Computer graphics.** Jobs in computer-aided design and imagery will greatly increase. Industries from manufacturing to fashion to video currently use computer graphics.
- **Information technology.** Fiber optics, the Internet, telecommunications, and other fast-growing areas of information technology will mean a far-reaching expansion of opportunities in this field.
- **Biotechnology.** This brave new world will offer opportunities for people with backgrounds in biology, chemistry, and engineering.
- **Lasers.** With lasers being increasingly used in areas such as communications, health care, and manufacturing, workers with knowledge about them and their use will be in demand.

Experts also say we are shifting from a manufacturing-based economy to a service-based economy, and that more and more jobs will be technical and computer oriented—requiring technical training, rather than a college degree.

Whereas we once looked to big corporations for good jobs and job security, predictions are that small businesses, which can act quickly to implement new ideas and technology, will become increasingly important as employers.

Which of Those Job Areas Is for Me?

While you'll want to consider these predictions as you decide what job to seek, you shouldn't get into a particular field just because it has good growth potential. If none of the fast-growing areas listed above holds the slightest appeal for you, you won't be happy or successful choosing one. Despite the field's potential for growth, it makes no sense to seek a job in robotics if you have no patience for or interest in technology.

There are two key things to consider when choosing a job or career: your interests and your strengths. It only makes sense that if you're wild about food and cooking, you consider a career as a chef or in another area of food service. On the other hand, it makes no sense at all to consider a job as a landscape architect if you hate to be outside, are allergic to grasses, and have no interest in or knowledge about plants.

Take a hard, honest look at yourself: skills, interests, strengths, and weaknesses. Describe your perfect job, including the job description, the salary, the hours, and so on. Specify a particular field or industry in which you'd like to work, and then assess what jobs are available in your local area. Will a new job necessitate a move, and are you willing to do that?

Seek help from your college career center or another source of assistance. Talk to people in different careers to get a better understanding of what's involved in their jobs. Many books have been written about finding the right job, and many Internet sites can be helpful. The better idea you have of the kind of job you want, the easier it will be to identify that job when it comes along.

FINDING OUT WHAT'S AVAILABLE

Once you've determined what kind of job you want, you have to find the position that's right for you—and available. This is where networking comes in. Networking is the single most effective means of locating a job, and other methods of job searching work best when done in conjunction with networking.

Typically, many people depend on the classified ads for job listings. They are an okay place to start, but don't think that you're getting a full picture of what's available by perusing the help-wanted section of the newspaper. Using an employment agency is another traditional job-seeking tool, and some people find success. Keep in mind, though, that relatively few jobs get listed with agencies. You're not getting the whole employment picture there either, and the agency may require an advance fee.

The Internet is becoming helpful for job hunters and can be a valuable tool. Most of Chapter 15 is devoted to telling you how to use the Internet to your advantage.

Targeting and making contact directly with a company that you know has job openings or may have openings soon is another method of job hunting. You have to know how to do this properly, and it's most effectively done in combination with networking.

As mentioned earlier, networking is the most effective job-search method. That's not to rule out the other methods. They serve a purpose, especially if they're used in combination with networking. We'll learn more about other methods, their advantages and disadvantages, in Chapter 2. Just remember that there are a lot more ways to look for a job than scanning the classified ads.

CONTACTING AN EMPLOYER

After you've identified an interesting job position, you have to let the employer know you're out there and that you're the right person for the job. There are different ways of doing this, but the most common is to send a résumé accompanied by a cover letter. Together, your résumé and cover letter serve as your calling card.

Your Résumé and Cover Letter

These pieces introduce you to a prospective employer, who makes immediate assumptions from what he or she reads. It's estimated that a busy employer spends no more than half a minute deciding whether a résumé is worth keeping—precious little time to make a good impression! Needless to say, it's vitally important to have a good résumé and know how to write a snappy cover letter that is tailored to the position offered and to the company offering it.

Here are some of employers' most common gripes concerning the résumés they receive:

- **Some material is irrelevant.** A potential employer doesn't need to know that you enjoy doing needlepoint and riding horses in your spare time if those activities have nothing to do with the job you are soliciting.
- **The résumé just doesn't look nice.** Poor layout, typing, and reproduction all make a bad impression on a potential employer. Don't skimp to save a few pennies!
- **There's too much (or too little) information.** Do you really need to mention your stint as secretary of your local bicycling club? Not unless you're applying for a secretarial job or to a bicycle shop.
- **Grammar, punctuation, and spelling errors abound.** Don't depend on your computer's spell-check feature to catch all the errors; if you type "than" instead of "that," you'll have an incorrect sentence but not a misspelled word. Check, double check, then have someone else check your work.

- **The prospective employee comes across as boastful, misleading, or down-right dishonest.** Any one of these faults isn't going to endear you to the person who is hiring. Think twice about mentioning that you were the head cheerleader for three years straight. Don't exaggerate, and don't embellish.
- **Gaps of time are unaccounted for and left unexplained.** You really do have to list what you were doing for nine months between college and your first job, even if it was hitchhiking around Europe!

These gripes aren't here to scare you; they show that there are a lot of other people out there with the same goal as you—to get a job. Chances are that some of those people are going to be looking at the same jobs you are. You have to make a strong positive impression, and you have to do it fast. Your résumé and cover letter can do that for you.

Poorly written résumés and cover letters are likely to eliminate you from the competition before you ever get a chance to play. Don't underestimate the competition, either. It's estimated that more than 100 million résumés are mailed out each year in this country; top companies report that they receive between 25,000 and 50,000 résumés annually.

BE CAREFUL!

If you're tempted to take shortcuts with your résumé or a cover letter—don't! Be sure you've checked everything, and then check it again and again. Ask a friend or family member to read through, for good measure.

I know a woman who was asked to send a résumé after talking on the telephone to a partner at a small advertising agency about an available position there. In her cover letter, she addressed the partner by name. Unfortunately, she used the wrong name! She later said she had had doubts about the name and had meant to verify it before sending the letter but didn't.

The partner at the agency was not impressed by the woman's carelessness. Needless to say, she didn't get the job.

Résumé Format

There are all kinds of résumé styles, and entire books are devoted to teaching you the art of writing them. I won't go into them all here, but some tips are worth mentioning.

Unless you're extremely uncomfortable using a word processor, you can prob-ably do your own résumé and it will look just fine. Look for a good résumé writ-ing software program if there isn't one already included with your computer or software. These programs walk you through the steps of creating a résumé, allow-ing you to tailor it to suit your needs. If you really don't think you can do it your-self, many services will do it for you—for a fee.

Here are some basic guidelines to consider when creating your résumé:

- **A standard résumé is one page long.** If you've worked only a short time or are looking for a first job, one page is probably enough. If you can't fit all the pertinent information on one page, feel free to use a second page—but make sure that it's truly relevant.
- **If you do use two pages**, run the résumé on the front and back of one page. This method is more professional and easier to handle than sheets of paper that are stapled together.
- **Leave a lot of white space.** You may be tempted to fill up the page with information, but it's important to leave a lot of white space between para-graphs and use wide margins. This format makes the résumé easier and more inviting to read and leaves the interviewer room to write notes.
- **Use high-quality bond paper in a conservative color** (white, off-white, gray, or beige). You'll attract attention—but probably not the kind you want—if you decide on neon green or fluorescent orange.
- **Print your résumé using a good-quality laser printer, or have it typeset.** Avoid using a printer that will make your résumé look unprofessional and/or mass produced.
- **Don't cut costs when preparing your résumé.** Using cheap paper or a poor-quality printer might save you a few dollars. However, the impression it makes (most likely a bad one) might even cost you a chance at a job.

What To Include in Your Résumé

Opening Section

Start your résumé with a good opening, a line or two often called the "objective." State your job goal specifically and succinctly. For example, if you're looking for a job as a market researcher, speak four languages, and have traveled extensively in other countries, you would do yourself a disservice to state your objective simply as, "To work as a market researcher." Instead, try something like, "To work in a specialized position requiring a multilingual researcher with extensive travel experience." This way, you've immediately set yourself apart from the crowd. You can almost guarantee the prospective employer will keep on reading.

Professional Experience

Follow your objective with a summary of your professional experience (which sounds better than "work history"). Account for all your time; employers are wary of unexplained time between positions. Start with your most recent job and work backward, giving three or four lines to each position. Try to relate how your previous work will be valuable to the position for which you're applying.

Specify your accomplishments, either in this section or in a separate one. If you saved your company half a million dollars by figuring out a more efficient way to wrap hamburgers, by all means, say so! Under no circumstances, however, should you include information that is untrue or exaggerated. Remember, all information can be verified, and exaggerating, embellishing the truth, or lying on your résumé is not going to impress a prospective employer.

Education

In addition to your college, technical, or other degrees, include any applicable certificates or licenses you've earned. If your degree is not related to the job you're seeking, think about the skills you have as a result of the degree and show how those skills apply to the field you want to enter.

Again, don't forget to include significant accomplishments. If you graduated *summa cum laude* while juggling the responsibilities of team captain, newspaper editor, and student body president, say so! Just don't make a big deal about it, and don't embellish it.

Closing Section

Like the opening section, your closing should include something that will set you apart from other candidates. Good beginnings and endings are vital, because they are best remembered. If you climbed Mount Everest the summer you graduated from college, this might be the place to mention it.

Who will remember the standard "References available on request"? Try to come up with something interesting (and truthful) to round out your great résumé.

The Interview

Job search excitement shifts into high gear when you start scheduling interviews. You finally will have the chance to tell that prospective employer, face to face, why you would be a great asset to her company.

If the mere thought of this prospect makes you decidedly nervous, you're not alone. Job interviews don't qualify as relaxing pastimes. They are much less stressful than anticipated, however, when you have properly prepared. Interviewers say they're repeatedly astounded by the number of applicants who come to interviews completely unprepared.

Preparation for the Big Day

Much information is available about interviewing, so I won't spend too much time on it here. Here are some important guidelines worth emphasizing:

- **Learn as much as you can about the company** before your interview. Talk to people you know who work there. If the company has a Web site or publishes written information, check it out. Try to get some idea of the company's philosophies and attitudes as well as its product line, locations, and size.
- **Find out where you're meeting and with whom.** If you're not sure how to get to the interview location, find out before the day of the appointment—you won't impress anyone by arriving 20 minutes late. Be sure you know the name of your interviewer and how to pronounce it.
- **Think about questions that the interviewer might ask** before the day of your appointment. Take time to formulate answers that take into account your strengths, weaknesses, and background. Then, practice them!
- **Make a good first impression.** Dress conservatively, be courteous, and try to relax. Your outfit should be clean and neatly ironed, and your shoes polished. Even if you know that the company's dress code is rather casual, wear a suit or a nice blazer with pants or a skirt. Dressing up shows respect and professionalism, and you'll have lots of opportunity to "dress down" once you get the job.
- **Make an effort to ask questions.** Interviewers often complain that interviewees don't ask enough questions, so prepare questions about the company, the job, the department, working environment, and so forth. The more information you get about the company, the better prepared you'll be to make a decision when you're offered the job.

- **Incorporate your achievements into your responses.** If the interviewer asks, "What would you do to increase the overall sales of the so-and-so department?" mention the successful strategy you implemented to increase overall sales in your last job. Be matter-of-fact, not boastful.

- **Follow the lead of your interviewer.** If she's a brisk, all-business, let's-get-to-the-point kind of person, follow her lead; keep your answers and questions concise and focused. If she's friendly and chatty, you do the same. We all tend to be more comfortable and open with people who are like us.

- **Don't talk about yourself too much.** Perhaps nothing turns off an interviewer more.

- **Answer the questions you're asked**, but don't volunteer information that doesn't apply to the job. Do, however, ask your interviewer questions about herself if the opportunity arises. If you notice something interesting hanging on the wall, for instance, ask about it.

- **Don't hesitate to tell the interviewer that you're perfect for the job** if you think so. Say something like, "From what we've talked about today and all I've heard about this position and your company, I think I would be very happy here and could be a valuable member of your team."

Follow Up

Interviews are extremely important, but the job search is not over until you start your new job. You can enhance the impression you made at your interview by following up with the right kind of response.

Send a note to the interviewer no more than one week after your interview, thanking him or her for meeting with you and for taking the time to answer your questions. The main focus of your letter, however, should be to express your serious interest in the company and your enthusiasm about working there. Mention a plan or goal that was discussed during the interview, and offer a suggestion or two for how you could contribute to its success. For instance, if the company's goal is to increase its client base by 10 percent over the next year, tell how you could help to achieve that goal, or send along an article from a trade magazine about a company that achieved a similar goal. The idea is to act like you're already a member of the team. Hopefully, your prospective employer will soon become your new employer.

If you don't hear anything from the company in a week or so, send along something else pertaining to a topic discussed during your interview. Try not to get frustrated if you don't hear anything as quickly as you'd like. Assume the interviewer is busy with other things and hasn't had a chance to reply. A sluggish reply probably has nothing to do with you.

Instead, use some networking skills and get in touch with someone who works at the company. Has he heard anything? Has someone else been hired?

Looking for a job is hard work, but it doesn't have to be overwhelming, intimidating, or traumatic. The better you're prepared for a job search, the more successful you'll be.

Networking Notes

- Networking will make your job hunt—and many other areas of your life—a lot easier.
- Consider the rapid-growth areas of health care, robotics, computer graphics, information technology, biotechnology, and lasers when contemplating job possibilities.
- Your interests and strengths are the key factors to consider when choosing a career.
- Consider all available methods when trying to locate a job: classified ads, employment agencies, the Internet, direct targeting and contact, and especially networking.
- Your résumé should be neat and professional; include something special about you in the opening objective and/or closing section that the reader will remember.
- Prepare for a job interview by learning all you can about the company with which you're interviewing and by anticipating questions and answers.
- Always follow up after an interview with a thank-you note that also emphasizes your interest in and value to the company.

CHAPTER | 2

IF YOU'RE OUT THERE IN THE JOB MARKET, YOU'RE GONNA NEED A NETWORK

I f the words "job market" or the thought of being "in the job market" makes you break out in a rash, keep in mind that you're not alone. For many people, job hunting ranks along with root canals and federal income taxes on the continuum of life experiences. Few people actually enjoy job hunting, but it doesn't have to be an unpleasant experience.

There is no shame in being in the job market; it simply means that you're looking for a job. It doesn't indicate that you're damaged goods, not worth your salt, undependable, or down on your luck. You might be in the job market because you've lost your job and are looking for another. Or because you're just out of college, technical, or career school and are looking for your first job. Or because you're not sufficiently appreciated in your current job and are looking for a position that will maximize your skills and abilities. There are any number of reasons why you may be perfecting your résumé and brushing up on your interviewing skills.

Regardless of how you got in the job market, you have to be ready to ask for some help. Relax—this doesn't mean you have to go crawling to your brother-in-law's front door and beg him to introduce you to his golf partner, who happens to own an accounting firm. Nor does it mean you should frantically start calling everyone you've known from sixth grade on up to ask whether they have any hot job tips.

It *does* mean that you're going to need to do some well-planned, carefully thought-out networking.

LAYOFFS, DOWNSIZING, AND OTHER DIRTY WORDS

I've heard horror stories: executives who lost their jobs during the downsizing spree of the 1990s and spent three years working in McDonalds because they were unable to find other professional jobs; middle-management types who were laid off from one position and found another, only to be laid off again.

Whether it's due to downsizing, layoffs, job elimination, managed reductions, or old-fashioned firings, losing your job can be a devastating event. Losing your job displaces you and can take away your sense of who you are, experts say. We place great value on our jobs as indicators of our places within society. What we do is sometimes perceived to be as important as who we are.

Think about meeting somebody for the first time at a party, at school, at church, or at a neighbor's house. Typically, your conversation begins with introductions, followed by a few minutes of casual chatting. Then, one of you asks, "So, what kind of work are you in?" or "What do you do?" Our jobs give us a sense of identity. To go from having a job to not having a job can leave a person no longer knowing where he stands.

A job loss can, in a minute, make a person stop feeling like a breadwinner and start feeling like a burden. It is especially difficult for a person who is the primary or the sole earner for the family to lose a job. When not dealt with positively, job loss can cause feelings of isolation, fear, anger, loss of status, and depression.

When Kurt Smith (not his real name) lost his job after 16 years with the same company, he experienced a range of emotions. "It took a couple of days for it to sink in," he says. "I guess I was in shock or something. When I finally realized I wasn't going back to my job, I was furious. Then I got depressed, and I stayed depressed for a long time."

Kurt's reaction is fairly typical. Loss of a job can kick off a series of emotions much like those experienced with a traumatic event, such as the death of a loved one. It doesn't have to be that way, though. Striving to maintain a positive attitude after losing a job and while searching for a new one isn't always the easiest thing to do, but it's necessary and vital.

You're Not Alone

Nearly everyone knows someone who lost a job during the lean, mean years of downsizing. Several years ago, U.S. Labor Secretary Robert Reich advised American workers to adjust their thinking and accept that layoffs will happen. "Job security is a thing of the past," he said. "People are going to have to get used to the idea of involuntary separations—sometimes four, five, or six times during a career."

Being laid off or downsized doesn't mean you're a bad worker, a bad provider, or a bad person. The 1990s have nearly ended, and everybody knows that losing a job is a real possibility. There is no shame in being a victim of downsizing.

Susan Larson Williams, vice president for human resources at VF Corporation (one of the world's largest apparel manufacturers, with brand names including Lee, Wrangler, Vanity Fair, Healthtex, Jansport, Jantzen, Joe Boxer Jeans, and Red Kap), said her attitude toward unemployment has changed drastically during the past decade. "Ten years ago, I'd wonder what was wrong with a person who had been let go from a company after a long period of employment there," she said. "But now, I don't think twice if somebody's been downsized. It doesn't matter at all from a human resources standpoint."

Many people who have lost their jobs unintentionally make their situations bleaker than necessary by putting themselves in a form of self-imposed isolation. Shame, frustration, anger, or depression may cause them to withdraw at the very time it would be most beneficial to remain in touch and do some serious networking.

If you have lost your job and feel this urge to suffer in silence and alone—don't! You'll only prolong your job search and make your period of unemployment unpleasant. Getting out and talking to and meeting with people you know, and people they know—in other words, networking—will move your search along and keep you in the mainstream while you're looking.

OUT OF SCHOOL AND READY TO WORK

If you recently graduated from college or completed technical or other career training, congratulations! You've taken a big step toward your goal of having a successful and rewarding career. The next step toward beginning that career is finding a job.

If your degree or certification is in a technology-related field, congratulations again. Experts predict that more and more technically based and computer-oriented jobs will be created as we approach 2000. Such predictions are usually right on target.

Surveys show that many 1998 graduates with engineering and computer science majors were looking at job offers with starting salaries as high as $50,000. The number of engineering and computer science majors has decreased sharply as our economy shifts from an industrial base to a service information base. As a result, there has been a great demand for people trained in technology.

If you're not an engineering or computer science grad, don't despair. A survey conducted by the National Association of Colleges and Employers (NACE) showed that liberal arts majors will enjoy a trickle-down effect of the technology boom. "Liberal arts majors are attractive to employers because they come prepared with communication skills and the ability to learn technical skills," said Camille Luckenbaugh, director of employment information at NACE.

All in all, prospects are looking bright for recent grads starting out in the working world. Still, you'll do better with a little help from your network. What—you don't have one? No problem. By the end of this book, you'll be so well connected that you won't be able to leave your home without running into somebody who's in your network (okay, that's a bit exaggerated, but you get the point).

WORKING HERE, LOOKING ELSEWHERE

Of the three categories covered in this chapter, this category of job searcher is arguably the most desirable. It's safe to say that most people would prefer the security of having a job while they search for a new one. Granted, some adventurous souls might respond positively to the challenge of being unemployed and needing to find a new job fast, but having a job while you look for another definitely has some advantages.

The Good Things

If you are currently working, you can manage your job search differently than if you were unemployed. For example, you can

- **Be choosy.** You can look objectively at what comes along and have the option of waiting for a better offer. If you don't have a job and you need one, anything that comes along might look pretty good—even if it's not.

- **Go at your own pace.** You can be as aggressive or as laid back as you want, depending on how badly you want out of your current position. You are not under the constant pressure that joblessness often imposes.
- **Take care of finances.** Maybe you've set a target date to be out of the job you're in, regardless of whether you've found another position. Planning ahead allows you to get your finances in order, something you don't have a chance to do if you lose your job suddenly. You can try to increase your savings by 20 percent as you anticipate a job change and possibly a period of unemployment or maybe look at your savings and determine how long you can afford to be without an income.
- **Feel confident.** Not having to deal with emotional issues related to not having a job can make for a better attitude.

Being in the workplace while looking for another job also gives you some great opportunities for networking. You've got a built-in network if you choose to take advantage of it.

The Bad Things

There also are some disadvantages to job hunting while employed. For one thing, you have to make time in an already busy schedule. This may mean cutting back on or temporarily giving up some of your hobbies. After all, there are only so many hours in a day.

You also may have to sneak around the workplace if you don't want your intentions to come to the attention of your employer, and it is more difficult to go on interviews and make phone calls related to your job search when you're working.

The Toss-Ups

If you're unemployed and looking for a job, keep in mind that you have these last few situations to your advantage. You have more incentive, more time, and more flexibility to execute your job search than somebody who is looking for a job while employed.

If you are already working and looking for another job, consider yourself lucky. Many unemployed people would love to be in your position.

A WORD TO THE WISE

Never assume your current employer won't hear that you're looking for another job. He or she might have a better networking system than you think.

WHAT'S THE BOTTOM LINE?

Employed and looking, unemployed and looking, or never been employed and looking—regardless of your circumstances, there's a common denominator: You're in the job market, looking for a job. So, you're going to need a network to help you get to the people you need to know and to locate jobs. First, let's review some of the commonly used job-search tools.

Classified Ads

They are a reasonable starting point for locating a job, but if classified ads are the only tool you're using, don't expect to find the job you want right away.

Experts say only about 10 percent of people looking for jobs find them through classified ads and that only about 3 percent of all available jobs are listed there. In addition, it's not unusual for a classified job for a professional or executive position to generate 200 to 500 responses.

Many people are attracted to the classifieds because it makes job hunting a pretty sterile undertaking—no potentially uncomfortable face-to-face meetings (until interview time), no follow-up phone calls. You read an ad, reply with a letter and your résumé, and wait for a return letter or phone call. This passive approach may be particularly appealing to somebody who's recently lost his job and doesn't feel up to going out and making a lot of contacts, but it certainly is not the most effective way to find a job.

You should know that some jobs are listed in the classified ads only as a formality. On two occasions, my friend Sandy applied for a public relations job in our community. She was extremely well qualified for both jobs, one at the branch campus of a major university, the other with the local school district. She had extensive experience in public relations and knew a lot of people at the college and within the school district. She expected to be a final candidate for the jobs, at the very least, but she never even got interviews.

After she received form rejection letters, Sandy contacted some people she knew. She was told that although the jobs had been advertised, the positions had effectively been filled *before* the ads ran! Had Sandy done some networking before responding to the ads, she could have saved herself some time and aggravation. She also may have been able to find a way to make herself a viable candidate.

Classified ads can be useful because they give you an idea which companies are hiring. Perhaps other jobs with the same companies weren't advertised. If you see an ad for a job that looks great, go ahead and send a letter and your résumé. Follow up with a phone call in a week or so, but don't sit around waiting for an answer. Active is always better than passive when you're in the job market.

F.Y.I.

A Florida author, looking for a researcher for a project he had in Pennsylvania, placed a six-line classified ad in the *Reading Eagle*, a mid-sized daily newspaper. He was shocked when he got more than 150 replies to his small ad. "I couldn't believe that little ad generated such a big response," he says. "I sure got my money's worth."

Employment Agencies

An employment agency is another traditional job-seeking tool, but fewer than 10 percent of all professional, managerial, and executive positions are listed with agencies. In addition, surveys show that only a small percentage of people who register with an agency are ever placed in a job.

That's not to say that it's never warranted to register with an agency or professional recruiter; as with classified ads, you might get lucky and find something that fits. My point is that registering with an agency and then sitting back to wait is a passive means of job hunting that makes you dependent on somebody else.

Should you choose to use an employment agency or recruiter, remember that the agency's top priority is the interests of the employer. The agency is looking for the best person for a particular job for a particular employer. If you're chosen, can you be sure it's the best job for you?

If you go the agency route and are offered a position with a firm you know little or nothing about, be sure you ask some questions before you make a final decision: Why is the job being filled through an agency or a recruiter? Is it because it's a highly specialized job that would require extensive resources to fill? Or, has the employer acquired such a reputation that nobody wants to work for him, and nobody working there will recommend the job or the boss to anybody they know? It pays to find out the answers to such questions before you accept an offer.

The Internet

Experts say that more and more people are using the Internet to find jobs, and many sites post job openings. Because it's a new method of job hunting, there's not much data available yet about just how many people are finding jobs on the Internet. This tool is discussed much more extensively in Chapter 15, where you're given lots of Web sites to check out.

KNOWING WHICH JOB MARKET TO TARGET

Responding to classified ads and using employment agencies or recruiting firms will give you access to the *visible* job market. The trouble is, everybody else has access to it, too. What you really want to do is gain access to the other job market: the *hidden* market. It's estimated that more than 70 percent of all jobs are found in the hidden market. These are jobs that aren't advertised and maybe don't even exist yet!

Finding a job in the hidden market is more difficult than answering a classified ad and hoping for the best. It requires an active job search. It requires persistence, resourcefulness, confidence, and the ability to meet someone and ask for help. In short, it requires networking.

Contacting a Company Directly

There are two steps to this method: targeting a company for which you think you'd like to work, then making contact with someone in that company. This two-pronged approach is a great way of accessing the hidden job market, and it brings us face-to-face with networking. You can target companies on your own, but it is easier to do with input. It's almost certain, however, that you'll need help establishing direct contact with someone from the company. You're going to need to network.

Library searches, information from friends, and gut instinct are all means of identifying companies for which you think you'd like to work.

- Doing extensive library searches, you can check out statistics and facts on various companies. You'll get an idea which appeal to you, which don't, and which you want to pursue for possible job opportunities.
- Talk is cheap, but maybe you've heard different people mention on different occasions how much they like their jobs at the XYZ Company. The bosses

are great, the benefits are great, the pay is great, and the rest of the employees can't be beat. If the claims appear to be warranted and the company has positions in your field, then you should take a closer look.

- A company might appeal to you for some other reason—you like its logo, its environmental policy, or that it holds an annual golf outing to benefit handicapped kids. It's certainly advisable to get some concrete information before you launch a bid for a job there, but it's okay to follow your instincts. Just remember that they may not always be right.

After you've targeted an organization—regardless of how—your next step is to make direct contact with someone there.

Finding Somebody To Talk to

Go back to some of those people who've said how great the XYZ Company is and ask for more information. You might say something like, "I've heard you and several of your coworkers mention what how great XYZ Company is. I would love to talk to someone about the possibility of working there, but I've got to get my foot in the door. Do you know who I would see about that?"

Ideally, the XYZ employee will say something like, "Yes, you need to see the head of human resources and that happens to be me. We have several positions we're trying to fill right now and I'll be happy to talk with you at length about employment opportunities." If that happens, consider yourself next in line for the top lottery prize—you've hit the jackpot.

Realistically, the person you've asked is likely to give you a couple of names of people involved with hiring. It's not as good as meeting the head of human resources, but it's a start, and later you'll learn how to use that kind of information and make it work for you.

If you've targeted a company on your own and you don't know anybody who works there, you'll have to be a little bit creative. Can you think of somebody who *knows* someone who works there? Does your college have an alumni magazine that lists places of employment? If you're having trouble identifying a contact, just ask around. You'll be surprised at how soon you find someone who knows someone, especially if the company is local.

Once you have obtained the name of a contact person within a company, call and say what you want. Once you've made contact, you're on your way. Step by step, you'll learn how to introduce yourself to your contact and how to get that person to help you.

You're Doing It!

This method of locating a job—targeting an organization and making a contact within it—is a direct lead-in to networking. In fact, once you've contacted somebody to get information about the organization or the name of someone who works there, you've started networking.

It's safe to say that all job-search methods work better when used in conjunction with networking and that some methods don't work at all without it. This truth will become increasingly apparent as you learn more about job searching. You'll see very clearly that everyone looking for a job does better with the help and support of a network.

Networking Notes

- Losing a job can be a devastating experience, but it's important to maintain a positive attitude.
- If you've just graduated or are about to graduate from college, trade school, or technical school, your prospects of finding a job are good. They'll be even better when you start to use your network.
- Looking for a job when you are already employed has both advantages and disadvantages.
- Classified ads, employment agencies, the Internet, and direct contact are all tools used in job hunting, and every method works better in conjunction with networking.
- Once you start targeting companies and making contacts within them, you're networking!

CHAPTER | 3

"WHAT IS A NETWORK, AND WHAT CAN IT DO FOR ME?"

By now, you have learned about identifying and locating jobs and should understand the importance of networking when embarking on the Great Job Hunt. Just by asking some questions and establishing some connections, you have started to network. Now, it's time to define two important terms: network and networking.

In its basic form, a *network* is the people that you know and the people that they know. Think of it as a web, with strands connecting people who know each other. These connections criss-cross, forming an interwoven, interdependent structure. *Networking* is being able to locate a person within this web who can help you in a particular situation, with the understanding that that person may someday call on you for help. It allows you to take shortcuts and to cut through red tape to find a solution.

Some networkers have an aggressive, up-front, in-your-face style, and others are more subtle and laid back in their approach. That's natural—there's no one right way to network, because every networker has a different personality.

TWO STYLES, TWO SUCCESSES

Joe is one of those highly visible guys who seems to know everybody. He has contacts all over the city and well beyond—you know this because he tells you every time you see him. You assume it's true, because he's always shaking hands, writing down phone numbers, and meeting people for drinks. He once came through for you with a tip about one of your competitors going out of business, and you were able to get a couple of accounts out of the deal.

Then there's Jerry, a quiet, unassuming guy. He's friendly and a darned good listener, but he doesn't say too much. The only way you know that he's got great connections is because on two different occasions he called to tell you he'd heard about customers who were very unhappy with the service they were getting from your competitor. You were able to connect with the disgruntled customers, one of which became—and still is—a large account.

These very different styles can be equally effective in networking.

BE CAREFUL!

There's a fine line between aggressive and obnoxious—we all know people who continually cross that line. It's possible to come on too strong when you're networking, and if you do, you end up turning off the very people you're trying to get on your side.

IT'S WHAT YOU MAKE IT

It's important to understand that your network is a changing, living thing. If handled properly, your network will grow and expand. Your web will get bigger and stronger as you add people to it: people you meet directly, and the people you learn about from others in your network.

Along the same line, networking is not a one-time act but a process. Sure, when you hear a rumor about a job opening at XYZ Company and call somebody there, get your information, and hang up, that's a single act. Making a phone call doesn't make you an effective networker. Using your network often and to its fullest advantage is the ongoing process of networking, and that is what successful networkers have learned to do well.

Networking can be simple or complex. An example of *simple networking* is when you call your friend Charley over at the XYZ Company to find out whether the rumor you heard about a job opening in the accounting department is true. Charley tells you it was true, but the position was filled last week. You thank

Charley, tell him next time you'll follow up on rumors more promptly, and say goodbye.

Networking becomes *complex* when you call Charley about the job rumor and he says that he heard about it from Janey, who knows more about it than he does. He puts you in touch with Janey, who says she thinks the job has been filled, but she's not sure. She recommends that you call John, so you do. You tell John that Janey gave you his name, and you're looking for some information about a possible job opening in the accounting apartment. John tells you that job was filled last week, but Anne told John this morning that she's going to be leaving XYZ and they'll be looking for somebody to replace her. So, you thank John, ask him for Anne's number, and then call Anne. Anne tells you she will indeed be leaving and that you should send a résumé and letter immediately to Roger, the head of the accounting apartment. In addition, Anne, who is a well-respected and long-time employee, will tell Roger to expect your résumé. Now, in addition to your friend Charley, you've connected with Janey, John, Anne, and Roger at the XYZ Company.

The simple networking example involved one phone call to one person. Mission accomplished. You got the information you needed. In the complex networking example, however, several things happened. You got the information you were looking for, but you also made four new contacts along the way. You also found out more information than you were originally seeking. Complex networking is a more time-consuming and roundabout method of gathering information, but it often leads to new contacts and extra knowledge.

We have looked at networking primarily in terms of finding a job, but there are dozens of other situations in which you'll use your network—everything from finding the best babysitter to locating a good Italian restaurant in another city. Some of your most important networking efforts may have nothing to do with your career.

I'D LIKE YOU TO MEET...

George, an experienced real estate investor, says he networks so much he doesn't even think about it: "It's nothing for me to spend a couple of hours on the phone, looking for information about different projects or checking out something I heard somebody talking about. I hardly even think about it anymore. When I need to know something, I pick up the phone and find somebody who can tell me."

George says that his car phone is invaluable to his networking and that he also receives a lot of calls from others looking for information.

A WORD TO THE WISE

Smart networkers note the names and phone numbers of everyone they speak to, then add them to a card file. Smart networkers also send brief thank-you notes to people who provide information or referrals.

THE NATURALS... AND THE OTHERS

Networking comes naturally to some people. A networking style stems from personal style, so some people have an advantage; others have to work at it. With a little effort, everyone can be a successful networker.

Consider Carol. She keeps in touch with friends from junior high school, college, and her very first job. She is friendly with all her old boyfriends and still sends Christmas cards to their mothers. She chats now and then with her former bosses, most of whom have become friends. She's the first to arrive at class reunions and makes it a point to talk to everybody there, handing out business cards as she goes along. She knows all her neighbors and invites them, along with various other people she's met throughout the year, to a big party every Fourth of July.

Carol is an excellent networker because she networks all the time, without thinking about it. Networking is as natural to her as sleeping—she'd be lost without her contacts.

Donald, Carol's husband, tends to let relationships wither and die. He has few "old" friends, hasn't been to a class reunion in the 25 years since he graduated from high school, and can hardly remember the names of his college roommates. He's well-liked and respected by his coworkers but choosy about who he goes out for a beer with after work. He's just as happy staying home on a Saturday night as he is going to a party, and he prefers small dinner parties to Carol's huge events. He's worked at the same company for his entire career and pretty much stays within his department.

As you have surely figured out, Donald is not a natural networker. He's basically shy and doesn't enjoy being around people he doesn't know. If he had to find another job, he'd find it difficult to approach people for help.

Carol and Donald's personality profiles show a lot about their natural propensity to network (or not). When it comes to networking skills, Carol is way out in front. This doesn't make her a better person than Donald, simply a better networker.

Although some people are naturally inclined toward networking, the skills also can be learned. If networking seems like a frightening prospect, or if the thought of calling or approaching a person you don't know makes you cringe, then you'll have to work a little harder than a natural networker. It will take some time and effort to overcome some of those characteristics that are holding you back, but you *can* do it.

Nobody is saying that if you work on networking skills you won't be shy anymore, but you'll learn to manage your shyness so that it doesn't work against you. Let's take a look at those personality traits that can make networking difficult and find out what can be done to overcome them.

Are You a Natural Networker?

A natural networker usually is

- extroverted,
- confident,
- willing to take chances,
- a good listener, and
- interested in other people.

If you are not a natural networker, you may have to work to overcome

- shyness,
- lack of self-confidence,
- fear of failure,
- feeling uncomfortable around people you don't know well, and
- being uninterested in people you don't know.

Shyness

If you are shy, you are by no means alone. Nearly everyone has occasional bouts of the garden-variety kind of shyness, which causes blushing and stammering; an estimated 3 to 12 percent of the overall population suffers from extreme shyness (also known as social phobia). Although it's normally not as debilitating as extreme shyness, "normal" shyness can hinder your ability to be effective in social

I'D LIKE YOU TO MEET...

Christopher Flynn, an independent mortgage broker based in Reading, Pennsylvania, depends on networking skills to maintain contacts and relationships that are extremely important to his business. He is a natural networker.

Christopher can talk to anybody about anything, and he has a terrific memory for names, facts, and events (he also happens to be about 6'3", weighs well over 200 pounds, and has a terrific smile—making him extra memorable to people he meets). He partially attributes his ease with networking to his large Irish-Catholic family, which was the source of much activity when he was a child. People were coming and going constantly, he recalls, and his parents insisted that he and his siblings learn the right way to greet people and make small talk. "I really think it helped that I learned at an early age how to look an adult in the eye while I shook hands and said, 'Hello,'" Christopher says. "I've always been comfortable with meeting people and talking with people because of that."

and professional situations. Common situations that bring about shyness are making a speech and interacting with an authority figure, such as a boss.

Experts say that shyness is not a condition in itself but a learned response and a habit. Like nearly all habits, it can be broken if enough effort is applied. It is one way of reacting to a situation, experts say, not an inborn trait. It might have been learned at an early age from a parent or sibling, or it might have developed later in life.

The old adage that children outgrow shyness is not always true. In fact, the problem can worsen as they get older.

Many people who suffer from shyness, especially extreme shyness, try to lessen the condition by using alcohol or drugs. This behavior only masks the condition and does nothing to correct it. Even people who seek professional help for the problem—and most don't, because of fear of humiliation—often receive drugs but not the necessary treatment to treat the condition.

If you are extremely shy and find that it hinders your efforts at networking, you may need to seek help in overcoming your shyness from a counselor or psychologist. Self-help materials also are available. Request The Shyness Reading List, a list of self-help and research materials about shyness, by calling 650-851-2994. Read information about shyness and related topics on the Internet at http://www.shyness.com.

I'D LIKE YOU TO MEET...

Bonnie, a professional who works for a large health care provider, was thrilled with her new management position. Still, she was wary about attending the meetings and getting to know the people with whom she'd be working. She always had been shy, didn't particularly enjoy meeting people, and had trouble handling "small talk."

One day, Bonnie decided to try something at a dinner she had to attend that night. She pretended that she was the confident, outgoing person she had always admired and that the rest of the people at the dinner were like her—shy and introverted.

Bonnie found it easier to approach people when she told herself that they'd be grateful if she did. She says she actually had a good time and felt much less self-conscious than she usually did.

Lack of Self-Confidence

Self-confidence is believing that you can do whatever you set out to do: putting together a first-class report that will knock the socks off your boss, running a marathon, or planning and throwing a fabulous party that your friends will talk about for months. Of course, careful planning and preparation are involved in these efforts, too. It's naive to think you could go out and run a marathon if your sneakers haven't seen their way around your block for two years—all the self-confidence in the world won't propel you the 26 miles and 385 yards of the marathon route! However, if you've trained and prepared adequately, self-confidence might provide that extra boost you need to complete the race.

Let's talk business, though. Think about the most successful people you know. I'll bet that they don't sit around thinking about why their ideas won't work or feeling sorry for themselves because they've got a briefcase full of work on a Friday night. Successful people find ways to get things done because they think that they can. They finish projects and get their ideas recognized and implemented because they believe in themselves and in their abilities.

If you're not a particularly self-confident person, you may find it hard to speak up for yourself or promote yourself. Guess what? Those are extremely important aspects to networking. You have to be willing to market yourself positively to people you don't know and who don't know you. (More about that later.)

If you need to increase your self-confidence, there are ways to do that. Don Taylor writes "Minding Your Own Business," a nationally syndicated column that runs every week in almost 100 newspapers and business trade publications and also appears online. He suggests seven keys to developing self-confidence:

1. **Begin with a desire to succeed.** Those who really want to improve their skills and abilities will find ways to do so. As they do, their self-confidence will increase.

2. **Become an expert.** Self-confidence based on ability and knowledge is very convincing. It will make others believe in you.

3. **Don't worry about what others think—just do it.** Stay focused on doing, rather than worrying. Your fears will decrease as you achieve results.

4. **Take a long journey in short steps.** When we do a small thing well, our self-confidence increases. As a result, we can take on bigger, more demanding tasks.

5. **Aim high, and believe you can.** Set lofty standards and goals for your performance. Believe you can accomplish anything you set out to do.

6. **Act confident, and you will be confident.** Don't let people know that your hands are sweating and your knees are shaking as you begin your presentation. Appear confident, and they'll believe you are.

7. **Surround yourself with confident friends.** Confidence is catching. Friends with positive attitudes bolster our self-confidence and help us to become more successful.

F.Y.I.

Remember that the only obstacle to the Little Engine That Could was his thinking that he couldn't get up that hill. It has been well documented that your attitude plays a huge role in all areas of your life. Thinking "positive" makes a world of difference in your overall mind-set.

Fear of Failure

I can't think of anybody who would prefer to fail, if given the choice—but many people set themselves up for failure all the time. If you think that you can't do something, you set yourself up to fail; every time you dwell on a failure, you set yourself up to fail again. One important thing to remember is that *everybody fails sometimes.* Moms, ministers, and even bosses fail on a regular basis at things they try to do.

If you should not succeed, chalk it up to experience. Think of the experience as a learning exercise, and plan how you'll do things differently next time. When it comes to networking, you're going to log some failures—not everyone will be willing to let you in or help you out. The only real failure would be if you got discouraged and quit.

F.Y.I.

Baseball legend Babe Ruth hit 714 home runs during his career—but he struck out 1,330 times.

Walt Disney's theme parks have been a phenomenal success! He had to ask 300 banks for capital to fund his dream before one finally agreed.

Feeling Uncomfortable Around People You Don't Know

In some ways, this personality trait is related to shyness, but many people who aren't at all shy sometimes feel uncomfortable when they're with people they don't know. You might be perfectly comfortable and at ease when you're with your friends, coworkers, and family but become extremely uncomfortable around strangers.

Networking is going to require interaction with people you don't know. Try to remember that most people you contact will be happy to meet you and more than willing to help.

Being Uninterested in People You Don't Know

Did you ever meet somebody who made it perfectly clear that he couldn't care less about you and what you have to say? This guy looks all around the room—not at you—the entire time you're talking. He offers no feedback to anything you say, because he's not listening. And he'll abruptly cut you off and move on to someone else who he thinks might be more interesting, helpful, or whatever.

If you suffer from the don't-give-a-darn syndrome, you will not be a successful networker unless you change your attitude. The best networkers are genuinely interested in others and make that clear by listening to and asking questions about the person with whom they're speaking. They look at you when you talk and make you feel like you're the most important person in the world.

This ability comes naturally to some and never will be mastered by all. You can, however, improve your people skills by looking directly at people when they talk. Really concentrate on what they're saying, and ask questions when appropriate. Smile when greeting and saying goodbye. In addition to making you a better networker, these skills will bring you into contact with some interesting people.

A WORD TO THE WISE

Whatever your opinion of President Bill Clinton, there's no denying that the guy has something going for him. He has survived in a scandal that would have destroyed many a politician. People who have met him say he makes the person he's talking to feel special.

THE BENEFITS

Assume that networking will come naturally to you. If it doesn't, make up your mind to work on and overcome any of the qualities that might make it difficult. It will be worth it! Networking will make your career more successful and your life easier. It also will do the following:

- **Give you access to people you want to know.** Did you ever wish you could meet somebody but didn't know how to do it? When your network is in place, you should be able to find somebody who knows somebody who knows the person you want to meet. The interconnecting strands of the web may lead straight to that person.
- **Keep you in touch when you're out of the mainstream.** If you find yourself out of work or in a new work situation, you might feel disconnected. Keeping up with your network during times of transition is critical, because those people provide support and encouragement.
- **Offer continuous opportunities.** A good networker is always on the lookout for opportunities and finds them often. Because networking gives you access to many people, you're in a position to learn about opportunities that non-networkers would miss.

- **Let you help others.** As you get involved with networking, you'll quickly learn that it's a two-way street. You'll also learn that the benefits of helping someone can be as great as receiving help.
- **Allow you to pursue your interests.** Did you ever notice that the really interesting people are those who are interested in everything? They possess a sense of wonder about things. Networking gives you access to people who know about all kinds of things, from auto racing to Chinese history.

I hope you're starting to get a picture of how important and valuable networking is. If you suffer from shyness or any other trait that will get in the way of effective networking, start now to try to overcome it. Don't be discouraged—like anything else, networking will become easier and more comfortable as you gain experience.

I'D LIKE YOU TO MEET...

I'm fortunate to be a member of an informal networking group in the Reading, Pennsylvania, area. It's an interesting group of women who share a common piece of history. We all started as reporters at the *Reading Eagle/Times* at about the same time. We were young, single, and having a great time learning the newspaper business.

Soon, we all got married. Then kids came along. One by one, we left the newspaper, finding that a reporter's hours are a difficult mix with child care and domestic responsibilities.

We have stayed in touch, however, and many times when one of us was offered a job she couldn't take or didn't want, that job went to someone else in the group. Freelance work, especially, was shared among the members of this group. Even though most of us have moved into different careers by now, the network remains intact. This source of continuity, support, and connection has benefited each member.

Networking Notes

- Your network is the people that you know and the people that those people know.
- Networking is being able to locate a person in your network who can help you in a particular situation, with the understanding that you'll help him or her when the opportunity arises.
- Simple networking is easier, but not always better, than complex networking.
- Complex networking will expose you to more people and more opportunities than simple networking.
- There are different networking styles, and no one is right or wrong. However, natural networkers find the process easier than those who aren't natural networkers.
- Personal qualities such as confidence, a willingness to take chances, an outgoing personality, good listening skills, and interest in others will make it easier to network.
- Shyness, lack of self-confidence, fear of failure, discomfort around strangers, and lack of interest in others may make networking more difficult.
- Networking can make your career more successful and your life easier.

CHAPTER | 4

THINGS TO DO WHILE YOU BUILD YOUR NETWORK

In the chapters to come, you'll learn how to build a network from the ground up. While you're doing that, there are some things you can do to keep your job search on track.

One of the most important things to keep in mind throughout your job search is that you're in charge. You can have first-class interviewing skills and the best résumé around, but if you sit around waiting for somebody to tell you what to do (or worse, wait for them to do it for you), you'll probably be sitting around for a long time.

A network will do a lot of things for you—except find you a job. Certainly, one or more members of your network may be helpful, even instrumental, in helping you find a job, but the task is ultimately yours. You have to build your network and maintain contacts. A network won't help you if its members don't know what you're doing or when you might need information or help.

During your job search, you are your own boss. Treat your job search as your job; set regular hours to work at it, and take it seriously. Make the phone calls, schedule meetings, participate in interviews, follow up on those interviews, make more phone calls, and schedule more meetings. You must get motivated to do these things, then do them—even when you'd rather be doing something else.

The prospect of a hike in the woods on a beautiful fall day may seriously tempt you to cancel a meeting and lace up your boots. That's a nice idea, but unless you're lucky enough to meet some outdoorsy executive who happens to be looking for like-minded employees enjoying a little time on the hiking trail, such a diversion will not help you find a job.

A WORD TO THE WISE

A writer who networked her way out of a corporate setting into a lucrative freelance business advises job hunters to schedule as many meetings as possible into a short period of time. "If you spread your meetings out over a month or two, you'll lose any sense of connection," she says. "Try to meet with everyone you need to within a couple of weeks."

INFORMATIONAL INTERVIEWS

An informational interview is an arranged meeting with a person who works in a particular profession or at a particular company. More of a networking tactic than an actual job interview is, its purpose is to allow you to gather information from the person with whom you're meeting about the profession or company in which he or she works.

An informational interview can be an important tool in your job search and is as an effective means of networking. As opposed to a job interview, during which your goal is to sell yourself and your abilities to a prospective employer, an informational interview is a learning experience. It's important to keep informational interviews in the proper perspective.

In Chapter 2, we talked about making contact with a person within a company. The same tactics—identifying someone who works for a company and then writing or calling to introduce yourself —apply when you're targeting a person with whom you'd like to arrange an informational interview. If you've targeted a company for which you would like to work, try to set up an information-gathering meeting with someone already employed there.

BE CAREFUL!

An informational interview is not an opportunity to ask for a job. If you request an informational interview but use the opportunity to ask for a job, you'll put the person you came to meet with in an awkward position. He or she will likely feel taken advantage of and less than charitable toward you.

Getting an Interview with Someone You Know

If you know someone who works at the place you're interested in, go ahead and call. Your job should be easy, because you already have a contact. If this person has never liked you, you might want to reconsider your tactics, but even a casual acquaintance is usually willing to take a few minutes to talk about the place where he or she works.

The same theory applies if you've targeted an industry within which you'd like to find work. If you want to be an accountant, for instance, and your father's former college roommate, Roger, owns an accounting firm, go for it!

If this guy is "Uncle Roger" to you, take the initiative to call him yourself and set up a meeting. Make sure he knows it's for the purpose of gathering information, and you won't be putting him on the spot by asking for job. If you don't know Roger very well and don't feel comfortable calling him, ask your dad to call and break the ice for you. Then, you should set up the interview. After all, you're not some kid looking for a summer job.

When you first talk to Roger, thank him for taking the time to take your call—no matter how well you know him. It's perfectly acceptable to chit-chat a little with someone you know, but you don't want to take up too much time (remember, you're calling to ask for some more of his time). Get to the point fairly quickly, and make sure he understands that you're gathering information, not looking for him to give you a job. Try to nail down a day and time for your meeting before you hang up. If that's not possible, ask when you may call back to set a date for your meeting.

Don't lose your momentum after you set up the meeting. One informational interview does not a sound career education program make. Set up additional interviews while you prepare for the one already scheduled.

A WORD TO THE WISE

Susan Larson Williams, vice president for human resources at VF Corporation, says she's flattered when someone calls to request an informational interview and is happy to find time to meet with someone looking for insights. "If someone calls me for advice, I feel that he must respect me and respect the job I do. I'm happy to help someone like that."

Getting an Interview with Someone You Sort-of Know

If you don't know anyone who works in a particular field or for a certain company, think about whether you know someone who knows someone. Does your uncle have a friend in the accounting department of the big restaurant supply company where he works? If so, would he be willing to break the ice for you and either introduce you to his friend or tell his friend about you and ask whether you may call?

Let's assume that Uncle Bob *does* have a friend in the accounting department. His name is Frank, and Uncle Bob assures you that he's a swell guy. Uncle Bob came through for you and mentioned to Frank that you'd like to meet him. Frank said he'd be happy to talk with you.

Because Frank knows who you are and is expecting a call, you don't need to write an introductory letter. Simply get him on the phone, say who you are, remind him of your relationship to Bob, and thank him for taking your call. Set up a meeting time right away, if at all possible. If it's not, find out when you can call back to finalize your plans.

BE CAREFUL!

If you're too proud to ask someone you know to introduce you to a friend, get over it. The whole point of networking is to establish and maintain contact with people who can both help you and receive help from you. You can't network if you're too proud to ask for a favor.

Understandably, anyone would less than thrilled to hear from you if you were asking to borrow money; however, most people would be pleased to help you meet someone who could help you on your chosen career path.

Getting an Interview with Someone You Hope To Know

If you don't know anyone who works within a particular industry or for a company that interests you and you haven't been able to come up with any names from friends, family, or business directories, try this approach.

Make a list of the firms that are within a reasonable distance from your home. Call each company and request the name of the supervisor in the department that interests you. There—you've got some names. Keep in mind that names are not yet contacts, but they're a good start. Next, write some letters. In your letter, you'll need to

- introduce yourself,
- provide a little background,
- request a meeting, and
- say you'll follow up with a phone call in a week to see whether she's willing to schedule a meeting.

Follow up one week later with a phone call. Think about what you'll say before picking up the phone. If you're told that the person you are calling is unavailable, leave your name and phone number, but also say that you'll call back in a few days, just in case you cannot be reached.

If the person doesn't call back within a few days, by all means call again. When you're finally connected, your conversation should include the following:

- Give your name; say that you hope your letter was received.
- Remind him or her that the letter requested only 15 minutes of time for the purpose of learning more about your chosen profession.
- Emphasize that you're not requesting a job interview.
- Suggest several days and general times that you are available, then let him or her schedule the meeting.
- Repeat the date and time of the meeting to make sure you're both clear about it.

There you go—you've set up an informational interview! It isn't all that difficult. Most people will agree to meet with you if they believe you're straightforward about your intentions. Some people won't, but that's okay. If you send out enough introductory letters, the law of averages will work in your favor. Try not to become discouraged by the rejections that are sure to arise; remember that Walt Disney had to go to 300 banks before he was able to realize his dream!

F.Y.I.

Hot Connections: Family members, neighbors, and friends. These are the people you *know* are always glad to see you, hear from you, or help you.

Warm Connections: The families and good friends of your friends, friends of your family, and people you've met but don't know very well. You *believe* these people would be willing to see you, hear from you, or help you.

Cold Connections: People you've never met, who don't know you, and don't know of you. You *hope* these people would be willing to meet you and talk with you.

Bad Connections: The only bad connections are those you never make.

Preparing for the Interview

After you've scheduled your informational interviews, you'll have to prepare for them. No two interviews will be the same, because every person you meet will be different. Try not to approach an interview with preconceived notions of what it will be like, because then if it turns out differently from what you expect, it might be unsettling.

Your first task in preparing for an informational interview is to learn about the company and the person with whom you'll be meeting. If possible, get a copy of the company's annual report and study the pertinent facts. Take notes, and get familiar with the material.

Check your local library or another source for information about the company that may have appeared recently in newspapers or business journals. Pay special attention to articles that happen to mention the name of the person with whom you'll be meeting. Has he been promoted recently? Was she the company's representative in the latest United Way campaign?

Don't overlook the Internet as an information source. Check whether the company you're visiting has a Web site, and search for general information about the industry. Remember, you can't have too much information. It's far better to be over-prepared than under-prepared.

After you've gathered as much information as you can, decide how you'll present yourself to the professional with whom you'll be speaking. Your spoken overview, a well-thought-out summary of what you hope to accomplish in the interview and your hopes for your own career, will lay the groundwork for your meeting.

Essential Preparation

To have a successful informational interview, you must be ready for it. Doing a few things in advance will make all your efforts worthwhile.

- **Do your homework.** Get all the information you can about the person with whom you'll be meeting, the company, and the industry.
- **Prepare a brief oral overview.** This overview should outline your objectives for the interview and state your general career goals.
- **Write down your questions.** It's hard to remember everything you wanted to ask when you have limited time. Bring your list to the interview so you can ask the right questions to get the information you need. How you modify the questions will depend on who you're interviewing and the career field you're exploring. Here are some general questions you should tailor to meet your own needs:

What do you like best about your job?

What don't you like about your job?

Is your job challenging? Are you excited about coming to work?

How do you spend an average day?

Which specific skills and training are required for a job like yours?

Are any particular personal qualities helpful for a person in your position?

What motivated you to pursue this career?

Would you recommend this field to someone starting out or considering a change in careers?

What is the possibility for advancement in this business?

What is the salary range in this business?

Do you have an idea what direction this industry will take over the next 5 or 10 years?

If you were starting your career over, would you choose the one you're in? Why or why not?

How do you balance your personal life with your professional life?

Use your list as a rough guide. Some questions that seem appropriate before the interview might seem inappropriate once you meet the person. Coming up with questions will be easier if you know the professional and have a sense of his or her personality.

The Day of the Interview

Your contacts are made, the meeting is arranged, you've done your homework, and your questions are ready. It's time for your informational interview.

What to wear? Dress as if you were going to a job interview; it shows professionalism and respect for the person who is taking time to meet you. Conservative, clean, and neat clothing and shoes are your best bets.

Take along a notebook and several pens—you'll want to take notes, and it's poor form to have to ask for paper and pens. Bring a copy or two of your résumé, too. Don't be pushy with it, but if the person you meet with asks for a copy, it would be a shame not to have one with you.

Be on time! Assume that the person you're meeting is busy, and be respectful of his or her time. If your appointment is at 9 a.m., start out early enough to leave ample time for heavy traffic, bad weather, or other possible problems.

When you meet the person you have come to interview, introduce yourself and explain what you hope to accomplish. Thank him or her for taking the time to meet with you, and ask whether it's okay for you to take notes (you hope to have a number of these interviews and shouldn't trust your memory to keep all the information straight). Ask as many questions as you can, but remember that you've requested only 15 minutes of this person's time. If your conversation is going well and he or she doesn't appear to be in any hurry to end the interview, don't worry about going 5 or 10 minutes longer, but don't push it if you want to leave your contact on good terms.

To wrap up your meeting, ask whether the person you met with could give you two or three names of people in the field who might be willing to meet with you. You certainly appreciate the input from the interview you just finished, but you are curious to see whether others in the field offer different perspectives. Also mention that you'd appreciate it if he or she would keep you in mind if any job opportunities should arise in the next couple of months.

If the person you're interviewing seems anxious to bring the interview to an end, don't overstay your welcome. When you notice that he or she has just glanced at the clock for the third time, graciously say how helpful the talk has been, and be on your way.

Organize your notes of the meeting as soon after the interview as possible, and file the name, address, and phone number (along with any other pertinent information) of the person with whom you met. Follow up your informational interview with a brief thank-you note.

DON'T OVERLOOK OPPORTUNITIES IN YOUR WORKPLACE

If you're already working, you have a potential network at your workplace. It will need to be examined and cultivated, though, before it can work effectively for you.

If you go to work each day and talk only with the people in your department or immediate area, you're wasting a lot of potential connections. How do you go about zeroing in on what's going on? How do you determine who can help you either advance within the company or move on to a better job at another company? These topics can be touchy. You can't waltz up to your superior and ask whether he or she has heard about any job openings at a competing firm. You can, however, request a few minutes of his or her time.

Use the same approach as you would with any informational interview. Tell the person that you're trying to get a better idea of how other departments within the company operate so you can more fully understand the connections between them and your own department. If you request an informational interview with a higher-up in your own department, mention that it would be helpful to you to learn from someone in authority exactly how the department is run and what is expected of department members.

Treat your meeting seriously. Plan your questions ahead of time, and take notes. Ask pertinent questions that will make you appear interested and tuned-in to what's going on within the company.

Most people will welcome your interest and will be glad to talk to you. Keep one thing in mind as you go about your mission: Just because someone is in a position of authority doesn't mean he or she is secure and confident in that position. There's always the chance that the person you ask for information will see you as a threat—that is, someone trying to get his or her job. It's best to get an idea of a person's personality before you ask for an informational interview.

Informational interviews aren't the only ways of getting connected at work. Here are some other suggestions:

- **Take some classes that relate to your job.** Be sure your supervisor knows that you've taken the initiative to improve your skills and knowledge.

- **Attend company lunches, dinners, retirement and holiday parties, picnics, and other social events.** Use these occasions to meet the people you know you should know but have little opportunity to meet in the office.
- **Join the company softball (or other sport) team.** Don't skip the beer-and-pizza get-togethers after the games. Many a relationship has been forged through such extracurricular activities.
- **Attend trade shows, seminars, or conventions relating to your job.** Your boss is likely to be impressed when you ask whether you could attend the seminar on improving your communication skills, and you can use it as a networking opportunity. You'll be a two-time winner!
- **Volunteer to serve on or head any committees or task forces that are organized within your company.** Taking initiative shows that you're organized and motivated. It also connects you with other motivated people.
- **Recognize the upwardly mobile employees in your office, and gravitate toward them.** Get to know them, and ask them out for lunch. Don't be intimidated; everyone can use another friend.
- **Avoid the gossips, whiners, and snipers.** These people will only undermine your career success because they won't be experiencing much of their own.

BE CAREFUL!

Under no circumstances do you want to give the impression that you're after somebody's job. Ask the questions for which you want answers, but don't focus exclusively on the job of the person you're interviewing.

YOU'RE ON YOUR WAY

In learning about informational interviews, you have been learning about networking, too. You've learned to tap into the resources of people you know, the people they know, and people you didn't know at all.

If you have arranged for informational meetings with some people you didn't know, then you've been indoctrinated into the art of cold calling—one of the things many people dread most about networking. And you did it successfully!

Congratulations! That wasn't so bad, was it? From here, you're ready to begin the step-by-step process of building a network.

Networking Notes

- During your Great Job Hunt, you have to be your own boss. This position requires discipline and perseverance in order to be successful.
- Informational interviews are a valuable tool when job hunting but must be treated as opportunities to obtain information, not a job itself.
- Contact people you know or "sort-of" know and request an informational interview. Most people are happy to help.
- Getting an informational interview with someone you don't know is a little more complicated, but entirely possible and not all that difficult.
- Prepare thoroughly for an informational interview by learning all you can about the company and the person with whom you'll be meeting. Also prepare a short overview about yourself and a list of questions you hope to have answered.
- Treat an informational interview as seriously as you would a job interview by dressing professionally, arriving on time, being prepared and polite, and following up with a thank-you note.
- Use informational interviews to get information about the company for which you already work. There's always more to learn about other departments, company structure, long-range plans, and other topics.

CHAPTER | 5

BUILDING YOUR NETWORK FROM SQUARE ONE

Back in the idealized days of the 1950s, nearly everyone had a network. It was built in. Of course, nobody *called* it a network, but it was. Sit back, relax, and consider the following scenario.

THE TRADITIONAL STORY

They were high school sweethearts. Joe went off to college while Mary, who had taken a business course in school, went to work as a secretary at a local car dealership. She had been highly recommended by her high school business education teacher.

Joe graduated from college, came home, and got a job in the bank. Joe and Mary got married, moved into an apartment above the camera shop, and saved their money. They had a great social life—lots of parties, picnics, and other outings with their families, friends from high school, and the new friends they were making at work.

Mary worked until she became pregnant with Bobby. Joe did well at the bank and moved up quickly. They bought their house shortly before Kate was born. It was a nice house in a nice community near the schools. As the kids went from elementary to junior high to senior high school, Mary spent her time keeping house, volunteering on school committees, helping out with community projects, and caring for her and Joe's aging parents. Bobby and Kate had lots of friends, many of whose parents were long-time friends of Joe and Mary. Everybody knew everybody else.

Joe retired from the bank as a vice president when he was 64. His coworkers gave him a big party and a gold watch. All of his and Mary's friends were there—it seemed like the whole town turned out!

You get the idea. Joe and Mary lived in the same town their whole lives, except for Joe's stint at college. They had the same neighbors for 40 years, Joe worked at the same bank for 40 years, and their kids hung around with other kids from families Joe and Mary knew. They knew everybody. They had as solid a network as you could ask for, just because of the nature of their lives.

THE SITUATION TODAY

Most of us don't expect to stay with the same company for 40 years; we're more likely to move around six or seven times. Most of us won't stay in the same homes for 40 years, either.

Our kids will play with kids from families we'll have to get to know—families that have moved into the area from other towns, other states, and other countries. We might not even know our neighbors, seeing them only as they enter their homes at the end of the day. Front porches have given way to back patios in enclosed yards. The things that used to provide ready-made networks—stable neighborhoods, picnics in the park, and community parades—are pretty much things of the past. Even school committees and community projects have difficult times finding enough volunteers because both moms and dads are working long days away from home.

Our lives are fast. They change quickly and often. We need to work much harder at maintaining relationships because the people we know often don't stay put. We need to work at building our networks because they are no longer par for the course.

WHY START NOW?

Meeting the president of XYZ Company at a local chamber of commerce breakfast will be of little value if you can't remember his name or what you talked about. You have to keep track of the people you meet in a way that you can easily access that name and number later. A network list is that best way to do that. Just a little tip: Do not—I repeat, *do not*—rely on your memory, no matter how good you think it is!

As you begin to build your network, bear in mind that networking takes time and requires attention. It's like a plant or a pet: Treat it with care and nurture it, and it will grow to be beautiful and serve you faithfully. Neglect it for a few months, and it will either die or take off, looking for a better place to live.

A WORD TO THE WISE

My husband can remember almost every phone number he's ever dialed. It's an amazing talent. Unfortunately, he tends to forget what day he's supposed to help with a writing workshop in our daughter's class and that he has four parking tickets to pay—trivial things like that. Nevertheless, he prides himself on his memory!

Having a good memory is great, but no one can remember all the little details that clutter our lives. Some well-placed notes and reminders certainly wouldn't hurt anyone, and they just might help.

An Early Start is Better, but Any Start Is Good

The best time to lay the groundwork for your network is before you start looking for a job. Long before, if possible. Unfortunately, many people think about networking only when they start thinking about changing jobs or careers, or when they find themselves unexpectedly catapulted into the job market. If you start to build your network before you have an immediate need for it, you will have some significant advantages:

- **You'll be working proactively, rather than reactively.** This gives you the ability to work at your own pace, with a lot less pressure.
- **Working in advance gives you the opportunity to meet and establish a relationship with people before you need their help.** It's a lot easier to

approach someone with whom you'd like to network if you don't have to ask for a favor first thing.

- **You'll be ready when you do need the network in a job search or for any other reason.** It's a real comfort to be able to remember (or search your card file for) the name of somebody who can provide help when you need it.

If you're already in the job market and just starting to build a network, don't despair. There are plenty of other people out there in the same situation. Although it's not the most ideal scenario, you're still ahead of the game for recognizing your need and doing something about it. Other folks are doing nothing more than sitting at the kitchen table, reading classified ads.

BE CAREFUL!

Asking a person to help you find a job the very first time you meet him or her is difficult and certainly not an ideal situation. The person you've approached may feel pressured—even resentful. Sometimes this approach is absolutely necessary, but avoid it whenever possible.

THE ALL-IMPORTANT LISTS

If you're going to build a network, you're going to need a networking list. It's the first and most basic step to getting started.

Who should be on the list, you ask? Everybody you know—well, or not so well—who might be of help to you, and you to them. When you stop and think about it, you know a lot of people: family, friends, college roommates. You've got an aunt in upstate New York, and you are friendly with your college roommate's family. Start writing down the names, and you'll find that it's true—you know a lot of people. These people will make up your expanded network.

You probably don't meet or talk at length with more than maybe 15 or 20 people on any given day. Look to these people, those you see or talk to most frequently, as the heart of your network (your core network). Other people should be included in your core network, too; for example, you may not see or talk to family members (other than those you live with) every day, but they belong in your core network.

The following lists provide some *examples* of whom to include on your networking lists; they are not intended to limit you. Everyone has different sources for networking contacts. Maybe you love bicycling and have met lots of interesting people in bike shops, at races, and at your local bike club meetings. In addition to knowing lots of people who share your interest in bicycling, you have a great networking pool at your disposal.

Go ahead and brainstorm; write down all the names you can think of at one time. Then, stretch your mind a bit and extend that list to include the other folks you know. Take some time and include people from all segments of your life, and I'll bet you'll find you have quite a list.

Your Expanded Network

- Former coworkers and bosses
- Present or former teachers, professors, and instructors
- Extended family members and their families
- Families of friends
- Friends of friends
- Former classmates and their friends
- Members of your place of worship—especially those with whom you serve on committees
- Members of any groups that you belong to (professional, municipal, service, or social)
- People you know from the health club or the gym
- Fellow members of the softball league or other sports teams
- Parents of your children's schoolmates
- Neighbors
- Professional people you deal with
- Shopkeepers, restaurateurs, and others whose businesses you frequent

Your Core Network

- Immediate family
- Extended family (grandparents, aunts, uncles, cousins)
- Close friends
- Coworkers that you see and interact with frequently
- People in the same clubs or groups that you see and interact with frequently

---

F.Y.I.

Go into a magazine store sometime and take a look at the selection of periodicals. The diversity of subjects covered in magazines is astounding. There are magazines for everything and everybody! The variety of topics gives you an indication of the diverse interests of the general population and the many potential ways in which people connect.

NETWORKING EXERCISE

Get ready for a trip down memory lane—and come up with a whole list of potential networking contacts. Get a couple sheets of paper or a notebook and create a worksheet on which you can write the names of any organizations of which you've been a member during the past 10 years or so. Depending on your age, these could include Boy Scouts, Girl Scouts, high school clubs, your college yearbook staff, parent-teacher organizations, professional groups, municipal or school boards, and athletic groups. Note the approximate dates that you were a member.

After each organization name, write down the names of as many people you can remember who also were members. Don't worry if some are missing; just do the best you can. When you're finished, your worksheet will look something like our **Networking Worksheet**.

NETWORKING WORKSHEET

<u>Name of Organization</u>   <u>Membership Date</u>

150th Anniversary Committee for Evergreen Township   **1989–90**
Other Members: Jane Smith, Ray Smith (co-chair), Richard Wey, Diane Jones, Bob Jenkins, Henry Stokes, Dr. Steve Rand, Jenny Martin, Kate Brown, State Rep. John Jones (honorary member)

Berks County Hiking Club   **1992–95**
Other Members: Marcia White, Jeffrey Smith, Joe Musser, Kathy Murphy, Ryan Murphy, Barbara Lucas, Mike Lucas, Patty Wagner, Bob Hill, Maria Hill, Jerry Reppert, Janet Moses, Barbara Bessinger, Rick McKay, Joe Delp, Hannie Delp

The Schuylkill Valley Conservation Action Group   **1993–96**
Other Members: Ralph Freed, Pat Walch, John Fritz, Jenny Strank, Brian Lucas, Cindy Funk, Dr. Melissa Raymond, Thomas High, Brenda High, Kurt Peters, Leslie Wright, Ray Wright, Denny Keim, David Brown, Peter Jorgensen, James Jorgensen

Middle School Parent-Teacher Organization   **1996–97**
Other Members: Charlene Krick (president), Mary Readinger (vice president), Jessica Speck (secretary), Kimberly Taylor (treasurer), Judy Smith, Steve Reed, Melanie Addison, Becky Williams, Laura Bright, Nancy Zimmer, Christine Kovach, Michael Wilson, Sara Wilson, Pat Reedy, Kathy Kauffman, Todd Kennedy, Sharon Becker, Lucy Fegley, Sheila Mertz, Sue Pullman, John Dade

March of Dimes Fundraising Dinner Public Relations Committee   **1996–98**
Other Members: Greg Price, Grace Mack, Dave Homan, Martha Homan, Howie Hastings, Amanda Boyd, Stan Degler

The Sunday School Leaders of Good Hope Church   **1997–Present**
Other Members: Mike Keller, Sara McGowan, Dave Krebs, Adam Kraft, Peg Anderson, Dr. Richard Bossler, Rev. Gail O'Neil

Adding Them Up

When you've finished, take a few minutes to count the names you've come up with. If you've belonged to six different organizations during the past 10 years (some of you will have belonged to many more) and you averaged 10 names per organization, then you have 60 names to add to your list of potential contacts.

My list contains 77 names, which is perfectly feasible. Certainly, not every name will be a winner. People may have moved away, or died, or otherwise disappeared. Chances are, though, that most of the people you remember from these groups will still be around. Many of them may still be members of the same group or another group of similar interest.

Taking Stock

When you go back and take a look at your list, you'll notice some interesting things. In mine, three of the six groups (the anniversary committee, the conservation action group, and the Sunday school leaders) include the names of doctors: Dr. Richard Bossler is a Ph.D. and Drs. Steve Rand and Melissa Raymond are medical doctors. A state representative was a member of the anniversary committee (albeit an honorary member), and the Sunday school group includes a minister.

In later chapters, you'll learn exactly who your network should include. Suffice it to say, though, that these names would be a very good start.

A WORD TO THE WISE

Never underestimate the value of belonging to a variety of groups. Many a career opportunity has been discovered during after-service social hours at a place of worship or at the membership meeting of the Kiwanis Club.

PUT IT ALL TOGETHER

When you add the 60 or so names from your organization list, the 30 or so names from your core group, and the who-knows-how-many names from your expanded list, you're going to have a lot of names. Great! And these are just the people that you *do* know.

You'll learn a little later how to expand that list to include people you *don't* know. You're off to a fine start. Don't worry if your list seems short; you'll have plenty of chances to add to it. Don't worry if your list seems too long, either; some of these names won't ever get past the list stage. You will not have to contact all of the people on your list.

Getting Your List in Order

A list of more than 100 scribbled (or typed) names can be overwhelming. Hopefully, it also is growing. To make your prospective networking list more useable, you have to get organized.

How you organize your network is a personal decision. Some people use books, some use file cards. Many experienced networkers wouldn't think of using anything but card files, but that method requires a backup for travel. Many people are turning to computer programs especially designed for keeping your networking information up to date. The advantage is, whenever you're plugged in and logged on, your networking file is with you. Face it, it's easier to carry a laptop computer onto a plane than a desktop card file! Another advantage is that you can easily make copies of computer files, selected entries or entire directories. If you use your computer to track and keep your network, print it out and keep a copy saved to diskette—just in case.

Even if your networking lists are on paper, it's a good idea to have a back-up copy. Compiling all this information is time-consuming work. You'd hate to have to start from scratch if you lost your list!

Regardless of how you choose to organize your network lists, make sure that you have the basics (name, address, and phone number) right. You won't make a very good impression if your thoughtful note has the addressee's name misspelled or if the address is wrong, so the note never arrives.

I'D LIKE YOU TO MEET...

Susan Larson Williams, vice president for human resources at VF Corporation, says that long ago in her career, a friend advised her to get a Rolodex-brand card file. "She said I just had to have a Rolodex, so I went out and got one," Susan recalls. Her Rolodex now has a prominent spot on her desk, and she relies on it heavily. "It's full of notes about the people listed in it," she says. "I keep track of their kids and their career moves and things like that."

A favorite networking strategy that Susan uses is what she calls "the Rolodex spin": "I spin through the Rolodex and see who I haven't been in touch with for a while," she explains. "Then, I give them a call."

F.Y.I.

Maybe it's ingrained in me from those years of newspaper work, but I still prefer paper to computer screens. My personal networking system is a large variation of an address book. It allows plenty of room for not only name, address, phone, fax, and e-mail information but also all kinds of notes and reminders. I even carry photos of a few of my favorite networking pals. And yes, I do have a copy of it.

Getting Past the Basics

An article in this morning's newspaper predicted that sometime in the not-too-distant future, all newborns will be assigned a telephone number that they'll keep for their entire lives to save worrying about whether somebody's telephone number has changed. For now, get all the numbers you can. It's hard to keep up with people in this fast-paced society, and you never know when you'll need to get in touch with somebody, fast.

Besides names and addresses, you can include your contacts' e-mail addresses and fax, cellular phone, private, and vacation home phone numbers in your networking list. As important as all those numbers are, though, they don't tell you anything about the person. Jot down some notes about each person. Include such not-so-trivial information as

- where you met and when
- present job and employer and how long he or she has been there
- whether he or she is happy in that job
- birthday
- marital status
- significant other's name (if applicable)
- children's names, ages, and birthdays (if applicable)
- hobbies
- pets

Beth has an Old English sheepdog that she's crazy about, so make a note to yourself to check the local dog show results. Mark has season tickets for the Penn State games and is the Nittany Lions' number one fan, so it wouldn't hurt to send him a little note should Penn State happen to get to the Rose Bowl.

If there are people on your list with whom you do business—doctors, lawyers, realtors, hairdressers, barbers, accountants, dry cleaners—note the approximate frequency of your visits there. You might be surprised to realize you patronized the dry cleaner's shop six times in two months. Do the math—that's 36 visits a year—I'd say you're a pretty good customer. It doesn't hurt to know where you stand.

Prioritizing Your List

It's just common sense that some names on your list will be more valuable than others. A friend you met the summer you worked as a camp counselor in the Catskills is on your list, but you haven't seen her for 13 years and you've only corresponded once or twice. She obviously won't be as important a networking connection as someone you meet twice a month for lunch and brainstorming sessions.

It will serve you well to prioritize your list. Near the top of your list, put the names of the people that you see all the time, talk to frequently, or do a lot of business with. Also add the names of people whom you've helped out or who have helped you.

Prioritizing your list might seem like a daunting task, but you've already identified your core networking group, so you have a head start. Do what you can now, and let the rest of the prioritizing happen naturally. It will quickly become apparent who your primary contacts are.

THIS STUFF IS FOR THE BIRDS—OR IS IT?

Some people are put off by the concept of networking. They say it's an artificial means of keeping in touch with people, most of whom you don't care about in the first place. I say, "Not so!"

Look through the contacts you have, whatever your means of keeping track of them. (Before I got serious about networking and organized my contact list, I threw the business cards of everyone I met into a basket on the corner of my desk. I had a box, next to the basket, where I put cards and notes to which I wanted to respond.) If you don't have any records yet, just think about the contacts you have.

Isn't there value in keeping in touch with people who have touched your life, even if it was only briefly? What ever happened to your co-counselor from Camp Greenwood? And that man you talked with for hours during the flight to London, when you had just graduated from college—didn't you get his business card and learn that he owns a communications firm in North Carolina? Sending him a Christmas card is not only good business sense but also a nice way to remember your trip to London.

I have never regretted keeping in touch with someone, but I have some deep regrets about not doing it. Never assume that somebody doesn't want to hear from you.

Networking Notes

- Ready-made networks of family, long-time neighbors, and life-long friends and coworkers aren't available to many of us these days. Because of that, we've got to get busy and build our own networks.
- The best time to start building a network is long before you need it for something major, like finding a job.
- Your core network includes family, close friends and relatives, and coworkers and other people you see often and with whom you're in close contact.
- Your expanded network includes people you know casually, such as friends of friends and family, former coworkers, people you know from clubs, and shopkeepers and others with whom you do business.
- A list of your networking contacts is essential. It should include the names of people in your core network and your expanded network.
- You're likely to be surprised how many people are on your networking list, once you add them all up.
- Recognize that some people on your list will be of greater value to your network than others.

CHAPTER | 6

NETWORKING TOOLS YOU WILL NEED

Pens, notebooks, card files, calendar, address books, software, business cards, and stationery are networking tools that you can buy at an office supply store. Sincerity, a good memory, a great smile, a firm handshake, organization, and persistence, however, are just as important—but they can't be bought.

Some of these so-called tools seem too obvious to bother mentioning. I mean, you always have pens lying around, right? But have you ever found yourself without one at a critical moment? Like, when you've just met somebody who's offered to introduce you to the boss at the XYZ Company? If you're lucky, that person will either have a business card or lend you a pen. If not, you'll have to trust your memory until you can jot down the information.

If you are not prepared at a critical moment, then you come off as being unorganized and less-than-professional. That's not the impression you want to make.

THE MOST BASIC OF BASICS

Imagine this: You show up for your very first informational interview. You're really excited because the woman who's agreed to meet with you is a high-ranking member of the company, and you never imagined that she'd see you. You have your notebook and a list of questions ready. But are *you* ready?

As you search your pockets, your discomfort becomes increasingly noticeable. You're starting to sweat, and you're thoroughly disgusted with yourself. You wanted to make such a good impression, and you can't even find a pen. What a start! Fortunately, the person you came to interview is gracious and loans you a beautiful gold-plated pen. By this time, you're so rattled you can't even remember which question you wanted to ask first. You have to wonder what the interviewee is thinking. Some first impression!

What if you remember the pen but leave your notebook behind? You can dig through your briefcase in hopes of finding some scrap paper or a piece with one blank side. Or, you could ask the person you've come to interview if you could borrow a few sheets of paper.

If you notice that you've forgotten something before you enter the building, you could run into the nearest store for a legal pad or a ballpoint pen. If there's a long line at the checkout and the woman with a carriage full of items decides she's going to pay with a check, then you might as well kiss goodbye the possibility of being on time for your interview.

These dramatic scenarios are intended to show you that the little things—like making sure you have pens (test them to make sure that they work!) and paper (a pad with a firm back, so you can write on your lap if you need to)—really are important. It is conceivable to think you might not get a job because you don't have the best qualifications or you just haven't connected with the right people; it's inconceivable to think you might not get it because you forgot something to write with.

A FILING SYSTEM THAT FITS

There are all sorts of ways to organize personal files. The most important thing is to figure out a system that will allow you to get your hands on the information you need—fast.

As your network grows, your contact list will become increasingly more important. The whole point of networking is to be able to quickly contact the person you need to reach. Whatever your note-keeping system, it has to be organized in a way that makes sense to you.

When you start to make contacts, you might be surprised at what you've collected in your pockets or purse by the end of the day: business cards and scraps of paper with phone numbers and e-mail addresses scribbled on them. What are you going to do with it all?

Essentially, you have to set up a filing system. There are different ways of doing this, and you may have to try more than one method before you find which is best for you. Remember, no matter what method you choose, it'll be most valuable to you if you file your information carefully, consistently, and regularly.

In offices, there are two schools of thought concerning filing. The first advocates putting everything that needs to be filed into a holding place—a basket or a box, for example—until you have a batch of papers that need to be filed. The other claims it's better to file information as soon as you've processed it.

With networking, it's better to file your information immediately. How many times have you found a phone number jotted down on the back of a store receipt and had absolutely no idea who the number belonged to? Your records will be more accurate if you make them while the information is still fresh in your mind. Notes that are perfectly clear to you one day can look positively cryptic the next. Transfer whatever information you bring home with you onto a card, into a book, or into your computer database—whatever method you choose.

Card Files

In Chapter 5, I mentioned card files as a popular method of storing and organizing your networking information. Many people swear by card files, but as a novice networker, don't feel compelled to run out and buy one—there are other ways to get organized. If you have your heart set on a card file, though, take some time to decide which kind will work best for you. All card files are not alike.

You may be surprised to find that the Rolodex company manufactures at least 10 different kinds of card files. The Petite Card File, for example, holds 125 or 250 cards, depending on the style you choose. At the other end of the Rolodex spectrum is the Covered Swivel Card File, which comes with 500 cards and has room for more. Base prices range from about $6 to about $40, so if price is a consideration, think about what you really need. You may not require a locking cover, if a cover at all.

Nearly all Rolodexes come with cards that are $2\frac{1}{2} \times 4$ inches, but the fancy swivel model holds cards either $2\frac{1}{2} \times 4$ or 3×5 inches. Some people feel that these cards aren't large enough to hold all the information you'll want to record about the people you meet, but judging from the popularity of Rolodexes, most networkers find it sufficient.

A cheap alternative to the Rolodex-type card file is to buy a package of 3×5 inch recipe cards and a box to store them. Recipe boxes often come with dividers, and the cards come in several colors, so you can file the cards alphabetically and colored by town or kind of contact, for example—or however else is logical to you.

One down side to having your information stored in a large card file is that it has limited portability; it's not a good idea to take cards out of the file because of the possibility of losing or unintentionally destroying them.

A WORD TO THE WISE

Don't remove cards from your card file and carry them with you because you think you'll need them along the way or when you get to where you're going. Many a card containing valuable information has gone through the washing machine or been sent to the dry cleaner because it was mistakenly left in a pocket. Don't store them in a briefcase or a purse, either. It's just too easy to lose those small cards that you spent so much effort to acquire.

Copy the information you might need (name, phone number, address) when you go to meet with someone, for example, but don't risk having to watch your efforts go down the drain.

Other Organizers

A more portable option than a card file is to list your networking contacts in a book that you can store in your briefcase or carry with you. Day Runner makes several varieties of personal organizers with ample room for names, addresses, phone numbers, and extra information. Most organizers have at least one plastic page with sleeves in which to insert business cards until you transfer them to your list. You can even buy a business card wallet—it looks like a slim organizer—to store those cards that otherwise might get lost in a pocket.

As mentioned in Chapter 5, you also can buy software systems that will help you organize contact information. One such program is Goldmine Contact Manager from Elan Software. Goldmine allows you to plug in basic information about the members of your network and keep records of all phone and fax communications. The only down side is the price: The software costs close to $200, considerably more than a high-end card file.

Some networkers prefer full-sized filing cabinets to desktop card files. They actually keep a file folder on each networking source. Although this system may seem a bit cumbersome and inconvenient at first, there are some advantages to a full-sized system:

- Documents that would not fit in a desktop card file—letters and brochures, for example—can be easily stored in a file folder.
- When you go to an interview, you can take the pertinent file with you and leave the rest of your list safe at home.
- If you want to organize your file other than alphabetically, you have more flexibility with a file you design yourself.

F.Y.I.

Check whether your home computer came loaded with software that might be helpful. My Gateway PC came loaded with Microsoft Works, which contains an address book application with plenty of room to enter all sorts of information.

OTHER TOOLS YOU'LL NEED

After you've decided how to organize your lists, you'll have to think about a few more things. When you're networking for job leads and other information pertaining to your career, you can't afford to appear unprofessional. Consider adding the following to your list of required tools:

- Business cards
- Personalized stationery
- A quiet place for phone calls
- A telephone answering machine
- Business clothing

Business Cards

When someone asks you for your card, it just won't do any good to mutter about how you must have left them at home while you rummage around for a scrap of paper on which to jot down your name and phone number. You need to have it ready, and it has to look professional.

Format

Flip through all the business cards you've accumulated sometime. It's not only a good exercise to see if you can put faces to all those names but also a chance to observe different styles: black ink, colored ink; white cards, colored cards; rounded corners, square corners; logos, no logos; embossing, no embossing. Which styles appeal to you? Which seem most effective? Which do you remember the best?

Standard business card size is $3\frac{1}{2} \times 2$ inches, and most are printed horizontally. Some people have them printed vertically, cut oversized, or otherwise customized so their cards stand out among others. This method might be effective, but it also can be annoying and put you at a disadvantage. Imagine shuffling through a stack of cards. When you get to one that's vertical instead of horizontal, you have to turn the stack of cards around in your hand to read it. If an oversized card doesn't fit in the card holders of the people you're passing it out to, where will it end up? On a bulletin board, lost in a stack of papers, or tossed into the trash? Whether or not you use a nonstandard business card is up to you, but you might be better off making the card stand out with a really great logo or a catchy slogan.

Beware of trying to fit your life's history onto your business card. Too many words and numbers crammed into a tiny space do not make for easy reading. Also

---

I'D LIKE YOU TO MEET...

Barbara Turkington, an independent marketing consultant in Boston, often attends meetings or social events at which she meets people with whom she wants to stay in touch. To avoid appearing disorganized or unprepared, she keeps several business cards in her pocket whenever she's somewhere that she might need them.

"Nothing looks more awkward or unprofessional than fumbling through a purse, looking for a business card," Barbara says. "I always carry several in my pocket, so I can pull it out and hand it over on a moment's notice—even without taking my eyes off the person with whom I'm talking."

resist the temptation to include every telephone number or address at which you can be reached. Home, work, cell, car, fax, and toll-free numbers convey the message that the person listed is technologically well connected, but how will the holder of the card know where to try first? Keep your business card simple—name, street address, phone number (one that has an answering machine or service), and e-mail address should do it—and it will work more effectively for you.

If you're employed by a company that uses standard business cards, you won't have much say in what your card looks like. Do verify the accuracy of the information *before* whoever responsible for such things has your cards printed. Make sure your name is spelled properly and your title and phone number are correct.

A WORD TO THE WISE

If you don't want your current employer to know you're looking for a new job, hand out your company business cards judiciously. When you network and interview all over town, leaving your card behind wherever you go, your employer is surely going to hear about it.

To avoid an untimely confrontation with your employer, consider getting personal business cards.

Personal Business Cards

Whether you're just entering the job market or are otherwise out of work and looking for another, you should get your own business card. There are several ways to go about it. A print shop used to be about the only place to get business cards, but today you have more options.

Print Shop

A standard print shop will design a card for you or make one to your specifications. Call around for prices before you order, as they might vary significantly. Ask to see some samples to get an idea what kind of card stock the printer uses and what color and quality of paper and ink are available. If you already have personalized letterhead or note cards, you might be able to coordinate the color of your card with the color of your stationery.

Online

If you have access to the Internet, you have access to numerous companies from which you can order cards at good prices, and you're guaranteed to get them fast.

- **Jaycards** (http://www.jaycards.com): You can choose from a variety of card layouts, with or without logos. Cards come in white only. Base prices are $9 for 100 cards, $35 for 500 cards, and $65 for 1,000 cards.
- **Jancer Group** (http://www.ufindm.com): You can choose from 15 card colors, from conservative gray linen to pink astrobrite. The base price is $32 for 1,000 cards.
- **Business Cards—01** (http://www.qualityquick.com): Talk about fast! Send your information to this company and they'll design your card, format it, and download it to your computer. You print it on pre-perforated sheets of paper designed for making business cards, and you're done. Prices are not listed on the Web site.

A WORD TO THE WISE

The price per card decreases significantly when you order large quantities. For example, you often can get 1,000 cards at a price only slightly higher than that for 500 cards. Before you order thousands of business cards, though, ask yourself, "Am I likely to move soon? Is my phone number likely to change?" Young networkers are often in transition. They're finishing college, moving out of their parents' house, or changing apartments. Remember that 2,000 business cards will last a long time—no matter how much networking you do!

Home Computer

If you're a do-it-yourselfer with a computer and a printer, you can design and print your own business cards very inexpensively. Most newer versions of word processing programs have templates for business cards and have access to clip art. Also check any graphics software that came loaded on your computer; if you don't already have it, you can buy a software kit that includes templates for business cards as well as note cards, signs, greeting cards, labels, letterhead, and banners.

Pre-perforated card stock (from standard-size business cards to quarter-page postcards to half-page greeting cards) is available from office supply stores. For the best quality, be sure to get the right product for your printer—laser and inkjet printers require different paper products to reduce burning, curling, and color bleed.

Regardless of the route you take, remember to follow some simple guidelines when designing or ordering business cards:

- Use a standard card size except under special circumstances.
- List only necessary, relevant information.
- Check and double check that the information on your card is accurate and spelled correctly *before* the cards are printed.
- Include an attractive logo if you have one.

Personalized Stationery

Writing notes and letters is an important part of networking. Your correspondence will be a lot more impressive if it's done on personalized stationery.

Personalized note cards, letterhead, and envelopes are available from printers, at stationery stores, and on the Internet. Basically, the same rules that apply to business cards also apply to stationery. Keep your design uncluttered, and unless you've got a darned good reason to do otherwise, stick with conservative colors. Pink astrobrite will undoubtedly attract attention, but is it the kind of attention you want?

Also consider the paper quality. Paper comes in many different weights and finishes, all of which project an image. If you're looking to land a job as an environmental consultant, recycled paper might be a good choice for your personal stationery. If you're hoping to land a position in a prestigious law firm, choose a conservative white, ivory, or gray paper with a high cotton content.

A Quiet Place for Phone Calls

You've worked hard at making a contact. You sent a letter, followed up with a phone call, then played phone tag for a week and a half. Finally, you're sitting in your kitchen, talking on the phone with the accounting manager of the XYZ Company. He's making small talk, which you hope is leading up to scheduling a meeting. You figure that he's checking you out, trying to get an impression of what you're like. This is an important step for a networking novice. You know that there's a lot riding on this phone call.

It's late afternoon, and you think you've got the apartment to yourself, but wouldn't you know it—here comes your roommate, with two buddies and the dog. They're not even inside yet, and already you know you're in trouble. You completely lose your concentration as they barge in, banging the door and yelling as they make their way to the kitchen. The refrigerator door crashes open and they start grabbing sodas, not even noticing that you're on the phone. The dog is barking, and by this time, you have no idea what the accounting manager is saying. The phone call ends in disaster, and you don't get your meeting.

If this story sounds like it could happen to you, then you understand the importance of having a relatively soundproof place in which to make and receive phone calls. Everyone understands the occasional interruption, but it definitely sends the wrong message if you sound like you're in the middle of a party.

Telephone Answering Machine

Telephones are even more important to successful networking than letterhead and note cards. After all, networking would be a long, slow process if all took place via written correspondence.

If you can't hang out near the phone when you're expecting calls, then you'll need an answering machine that you leave on all the time. Answering machines or services have become so common that you really are at a disadvantage if you don't have one. There's no guarantee that a busy professional will find time to try again if there's no answer and no way to leave a message.

By the way, those cute messages with music playing in the background were great when you were in college but not when you're looking for a job or trying to locate networking contacts. Your outgoing message should be clear and professional. A favorite joke really is not appropriate.

Business Clothing

Beginning networkers typically don't have a closet full of designer business clothing, but one good suit is well worth the investment. First impressions are powerful, and they can be very good or very bad.

In addition to a suit (or a conservative pair of slacks and a sports coat for men, or a conservative dress or skirt and jacket for women), you will need to wear a clean, pressed shirt or blouse in a conservative color and well-polished shoes. An overall neatly groomed appearance is a must. Women should avoid revealing clothing and extremely high-heeled shoes—you're looking for a job, not a date. Men should always wear a tie.

THE ESSENTIAL, INDISPENSABLE TOOLS

We've covered the obvious tools that you'll need to start networking successfully. The intangible ones, though, are every bit as essential to your networking success.

- **Sincerity.** Sincerity is important, because people sense when someone is sincere and respond positively to it; conversely, when someone is not sincere, they respond negatively. Don't say things that you don't mean, and don't offer to do anything that you can't follow through.

- **Handshakes.** A firm, enthusiastic handshake says a lot about a person. You probably have shaken hands with someone whose handshake was as soft and limp as a dishrag. Didn't it convey a less-than-favorable impression about that person? A strong handshake indicates vitality and confidence, whereas a weak handshake indicates—well, weakness.

- **Smiles.** Like a good handshake, a smile says a lot about a person. Aren't you drawn to a person who has a great smile and shows it a lot? A smile radiates happiness and friendliness. Keep yours readily available!

- **Persistence.** Persistence is one of the most important networking tools you'll need. If you get frustrated because your efforts don't appear to be paying off, you'll lose your motivation. Instead, keep on plugging away, and eventually you will see the fruits of your labor. If you're not a naturally persistent person, this trait is one to work on.

Networking Notes

- You'll need several tools for networking. Some are more important than others.
- Little things—like having pens, paper, and business cards accessible when you need them—can make the difference between leaving a professional impression and an unprofessional one.
- To have an effective network, you have to organize your information in some way. Many people use card files, but find the option that works for you.
- Business cards are a must for networking and job hunting. Your best bet is to order a conservative style in a standard size, and don't clutter the card with irrelevant or unnecessary information.
- Personalized stationery is desirable for networking. If you design your own letterhead, be sure to print your stationery on high-quality paper appropriate for your printer.
- Create a quiet place in which to make and receive phone calls, and have a telephone answering machine or service take calls when you cannot.
- When you plan to meet someone who might be important to your network, dress the part. It shows respect and projects a professional image.
- The truly indispensable tools for networking—sincerity, a strong handshake, a great smile, and an extra measure of persistence—can't be bought in an office supply store.

CHAPTER | 7

FINDING EVEN MORE PEOPLE TO INCLUDE IN YOUR NETWORK

The very first people that you added to your networking list are people you love: your family and your best friends—the people with whom you share histories and share your life. Networking is not a heartless, calculated plan for squeezing favors out of everyone you know. A network is for the mutual benefit of its members.

Let's review possible networking sources, which were covered in Chapter 5. Those in your core network—immediate family, other close family, close friends, coworkers with whom you have frequent contact, and people in the same clubs and groups—don't require further explanation. Then, there's your expanded networking group—former coworkers and bosses, teachers, neighbors, parents of your kids' friends, members of your church, and lots of other folks. How can you use these resources to add even more people to your network?

ENLARGING YOUR EXPANDED NETWORK

There are a number of routes you can explore when you want to add more names to your networking lists. Some of the more obvious are

- your family's family,
- your family's friends,
- friends of friends,
- families of friends, and
- families of your children's friends.

Your Family's Family

I have a brother-in-law whose father is well connected in the land development business and whose brother is a dean at a major university. Is my brother-in-law's family my family? Technically not, but it's my sister's family, and that's close enough.

I make it a point to send Christmas cards to these extended family members, catch up with them when I see them at my sister's home, and invite them to large celebrations with extended family.

Your Family's Friends

Don't underestimate the power of connections! You might not even realize the connections you have through your family.

Take Pat, for example. She applied to her first-choice college, a small, respected private institution about 45 miles from home. Come spring, she was told she was near the top of the waiting list. The college had capped its enrollment, and Pat's grades and college board scores weren't quite high enough to push her into the first tier of accepted students. She was devastated.

Pat *really* wanted to go to that college. She was losing hope when her grandmother intervened on her behalf. Busy with her own life and plans, Pat had forgotten that her grandmother had a good friend who had worked in the admissions office of the college for as long as anyone could remember. In fact, Pat probably didn't even know her grandmother's friend's name. But her grandmother talked to her friend, who talked to someone at the college admissions office, and before you know it—Pat was notified that she had been accepted.

Friends of Friends

You've probably heard the saying, "Any friend of yours is a friend of mine." Well, that isn't always true, but it sure is worth a try. Friends are valuable bridges when you're networking and often can not only introduce you to new people but also reconnect you with friends who have grown apart.

For instance, I stay in fairly close contact with about 10 college friends. Each of them stays in touch with some people I knew in college but didn't keep up with afterward. The friendships I've maintained can be used as natural connections to reestablish contact with those people with whom I've lost touch.

Some of my college friends have established successful careers and are great members of my network (in addition to being valued friends). Some of their friends have been even more successful and would be valuable additions to my network. So, what to do? Consider Mike, for example, who was a casual friend in college. He was president of the student government association then. Now, he's a member of the state house of representatives, representing the district in which our college is located. I haven't kept in touch with Mike, but I know that Julie, my former roommate, has. When I drop a note to Mike, then follow up with a phone call, you can be sure I'm going to mention Julie's name and the fact that I was her roommate. Julie will be my natural connection to Mike, who I would like to include in my network.

I'D LIKE YOU TO MEET...

Susan Larson Williams, vice president for human resources at VF Corporation, was looking at a newsletter that her alma mater (Augustana College in Rock Island, Illinois) had sent out to graduates. One section listed names of people who other graduates said they would most like to hear from. A friend with whom Susan had lost contact had included her name on his list. It listed his e-mail address, so she e-mailed him immediately and reestablished contact.

Susan learned that her old friend is now vice president of a major advertising agency and has lots of contacts that could be valuable to her. In addition, she's enjoying getting reacquainted with a long-lost friend. Never pass up an opportunity to reestablish contact!

Families of Friends

This category is an often-overlooked source of potential network members. Think about your friends. Now think about their families. Any school board members? Doctors? Salespeople? Corporate officers? The families of your friends can be very important to you and your network, and you've got a distinct advantage: You have a positive connection.

Your friend's dad, who happens to own a good-sized accounting firm, probably won't deny you a chance to talk or network if you contact him and say, "Hello, Mr. Jones? This is Ted Myers. I'm a good friend of your son, Jake." Within the first 20 seconds of your conversation, you've established a bond. That bond is Jake.

Don't overlook the younger siblings of your friends. I have a good friend who has a brother 10 years younger. That was a big age difference when we were 20 and he was 10, but 20 years later, the kid brother is a hot-shot lawyer on his way up, and the age difference doesn't matter a bit.

Families of Your Children's Friends

If you have kids—or if you plan to someday—read this section! Parents of the kids that your kids go to school with, play sports with, or just hang out with can be great additions to your network. The parents of my daughter's third-grade classmates included a federal judge, a dentist, an auto mechanic, and a policeman. One student's grandfather was a retired congressman who attended many of the school art shows, book fairs, and other events. All of these people are valuable networking contacts, and we were able to meet and get to know each other at parents' nights and at school plays.

More Possibilities

There are even more possible routes if you go beyond the obvious. For example,

- your spouse's friends and coworkers,
- people you work with but don't know very well,
- former colleagues,
- members of the boards or committees on which you serve,
- people you meet at social events,
- members of your place of worship,
- professionals you deal with regularly,

- people whose businesses you patronize,
- neighbors, and
- teachers, professors, and instructors.

Your Spouse's Friends and Coworkers

In most marriages, there are friends of the couple, friends of the husband, and friends of the wife. Friends of the wife might be coworkers, school friends, attendees of the same exercise class or gym, members of a professional organization, or someone a mutual friend has introduced.

If the husband is a smart networker, he'll remember that Linda, who his wife knows from the gym, is an assistant district attorney and that Kathy, his wife's friend from high school, owns her own advertising agency. He also will be gracious when his wife invites friends to their house, regardless of whether he's in the mood for company.

People You Work with but Don't Know Very Well

This could be a very large or a very small group, depending on where you work. Even if you work at a huge corporation, you've got common ground with everybody else that works there, from the president on down.

Former Colleagues

As with current colleagues, you share common ground with people you used to work with. I know a group of former coworkers who meet once a year to celebrate their "escape" from what they call the "boss from hell." They have great fun telling old war stories, catching up, and bragging about what they've done since leaving their common place of employment.

Members of the Boards or Committees on Which You Serve

Public service is an important tool for networking, as well as a valuable means of "giving something back" and making a difference.

People You Meet at Social Events

Social events are meant to be pleasurable, but they're also some of the very best opportunities for networking. Parties, weddings, picnics, dances, and luncheons give you the opportunity to relate with people on different levels than you do at work, school, or church or in other situations. They also put you in touch with people you haven't met before. When our friend John got married, we were

I'D LIKE YOU TO MEET...

A stay-at-home mom of three young boys, Janet Stokes was recently elected to her district's school board. Suddenly, her days of doing laundry, taking care of the house, and watching the kids are being interrupted by school district couriers in and out of her driveway, dropping off the latest confidential documents.

Janet has installed her first answering machine so she won't miss calls from other board members, school officials, and district residents. She spends a good deal of time catching up with people on the phone and tries to have lunch once a week at the restaurant where the township movers and shakers eat.

Although Janet's life is busier since she started her service on the school board, it is also far more interesting. This new responsibility has given her some great contacts and is teaching her the fine art of negotiation (e.g., "If I vote for your pet project, what can you do for me?").

expecting a good time but didn't realize the wedding reception would be as interesting as it was.

In addition to being a colorful character, John is a long-time political reporter. As a result, the wedding reception, held in the home of the bride's brother, was well attended by state senators, state representatives, local politicians, judges, and the like. It was a great chance to sit and talk with these people in a relaxed setting. You can be sure there was some first-rate networking occurring at that event!

Members of Your Place of Worship

Regardless of your religion, if you attend services with any regularity, you'll meet a lot of people. Although networking shouldn't be your first priority where and when you choose to worship, it's a nice side benefit. Belonging to a community of believers immediately gives you something in common. Shouldn't people help each other when they can?

Think about the people you know from your church, synagogue, mosque, or other place of worship and what connections they might have through their jobs, appointments, or interests. In my church's directory are doctors, dentists, police detectives, owners of car dealerships, college professors and administrators, business executives (working and retired), lawyers, craftspeople, nurses, the owner of an advertising agency, teachers (mostly from the schools that my kids attend), school administrators, musicians, local officials, caterers, a restaurant owner, marathon runners, and many other interesting people.

BE CAREFUL!

Don't join any organization, especially a place of worship, with the primary purpose of meeting people who can advance your career or other interests. This kind of behavior is immediately apparent to the other members and causes great resentment among the community.

Professionals You Deal with Regularly

You may already have connections with a doctor, a lawyer, and an accountant—you provide them with your business and a check, they provide you with their services. Because professionals carry some weight in our society, they can be very helpful in situations other than those you pay them for.

I have asked my lawyer for references on several occasions, and he's always come through. He's well known around town, and a reference from him sure doesn't hurt. When I need specific medical information for something I'm writing or researching, I call my doctor, who happens to be highly regarded in various medical associations. It sometimes takes a little while, but she always has been able to oblige.

People Whose Businesses You Patronize

If the old "I'll help you out if you help me out" theory is true, it certainly should be applicable with this group of potential networking sources. As a former newspaper reporter, I often had to ask around for information about one thing or another. You can bet that some of my first calls or visits were to the owners and employees of shops, restaurants, and other businesses where I was a customer. Why? Because these people are in the mainstream and know what's going on around town, and because they usually were willing to give me information because I was a customer they knew.

These relationships were mutually beneficial. Don't overlook other customers who patronize the same businesses, either. If you happen to drop off your dry cleaning every Tuesday morning before work and another woman drops hers off at the same time, you have an opportunity to get to know her. Never overlook a chance to get to know someone.

Neighbors

Neighbors are an often-overlooked category of networking possibilities—and for a good reason. We see our neighbors when we're at home, that is, when we're relaxing, out of business mode, in jeans and sneakers instead of a business suit and wing tips. Networking with your neighbors, you can find out who is the best plumber around, where you can find a landscaper who will deliver mulch without it costing a week's salary, what caused the power outage for an hour Friday night, and which hospital another neighbor, Mrs. Jones, is in.

Do you know the people who live on your street? How about at least the ones on either side and directly in front and behind you? They could be business hot shots, movers and shakers, or rock musicians. If you don't know, then maybe it's time to fire up the barbecue and invite them over. Neighbors are a great source of local information who should not be overlooked as possible career networking sources.

Teachers, Professors, and Instructors

Present and former teachers, professors, and instructors have all kinds of information and good connections. They also can be pretty wonderful people. I've kept in contact with a professor from my college since I graduated nearly 20 years ago. We have become very good friends and have gotten to know each other well. I've called on him numerous times over the years for information, references, connections, and inspiration.

Last year I was able to repay my friend the professor in a big way: I introduced him to another good friend. It was love at first sight, and my friends are about to be married. Guess who's the bridesmaid? Now you see what networking can do!

ESSENTIALS FOR YOUR NETWORKING LIST

Emergencies will happen. We usually are not ready for them, but they happen anyway. Some emergencies are life threatening. Some are inconvenient. Some are heartbreaking.

You can handle any emergency better if you are prepared for it. I don't mean the kind of preparation you do when you install a fire extinguisher in your kitchen, although that's a highly advisable move. I mean the preparation you do when you build your network.

If your network has you connected with people who can help you through an emergency, you'll be better off when they happen. Any parent whose child has ever awakened at night burning with fever, crying, coughing, and unable to catch a breath would trade the next promotion at work for the comfort of a trusted pediatrician who will talk to you on the phone, reassure you that your child will be okay, and prescribe croup medicine from the all-night pharmacy. Anyone who's ever been unexpectedly called away on a family or business emergency will remember with gratitude the travel agent who managed to get nonstop tickets at the last minute to get across the country in record time.

The people who are essential to your network will depend on your circumstances—what's essential to my list may not be essential to yours. You think it's absolutely necessary to have a top personal trainer in your network; I'd rather have a high-ranking school official on mine. An elderly person might want to be on a first-name basis with the dispatcher at the emergency services center, and parents of teenagers might want to know a cop with some clout who will check out parties, keep an eye out for drugs, and report who their kids hang out with.

Depending on where you are in life, your essential network members might include a lawyer (perhaps a divorce lawyer), a banker, a representative of a good nursing or retirement home, a dentist, a real estate agent, the maitre d' of your town's best restaurant, the superintendent of your children's school district, a public relations (damage control) professional, a therapist, or a wedding planner. If you are a home owner and have had a pipe burst and your water shut down, you know it's important to have a good plumber; if your electric oven once quit on you without warning on the day of your biggest party of the year, then an electrician is a necessary contact.

A computer whiz is absolutely essential on my networking list—someone who can fix any problem fast. Sure, I could send the thing back to the manufacturer and sit around for two or three weeks until it comes back, or I could rent a computer that I'm not used to and probably doesn't run the same way as mine. Instead, I've found a computer guy who comes to my house and fixes my computer while I wait. He's a must-have in my network.

It's helpful to have connections with a local official or two. When my neighbor was chairman of the township board of commissioners, our street was the first one in the area plowed after a snowstorm. Our gutters were swept regularly, and our streets were free of potholes for two years. Later, the same neighbor was elected to the school board, where he was instrumental in having our daughter placed in the class with the teacher that everyone wants their kids to have.

There's one more person you might not think about—or might not want to think about—for your network: a funeral director. A sudden death is a horrible thing. Nothing is going to make the experience easy, but a good funeral director can make a big difference. Look for someone you know, who knows you. Someone who will provide genuine comfort instead of empty words. Make sure you can trust this person to give you the service you want at a fair price, not talk you into buying things you don't need or want.

I'D LIKE YOU TO MEET...

Bob Alspach, the tried and true auto mechanic to my 10-year-old Volvo station wagon, is quite a networker. I met him at a local restaurant, where he used to eat breakfast every morning. He approached me in the parking lot and started asking questions about my car: "What year is it? Do you like it? Do you have any problems with it?" As it happened, the answer to the last question was yes—lots of problems. Bob handed me his card, invited me to come by his shop, and we've been doing business ever since.

BUILD TODAY WHAT YOU'LL NEED TOMORROW

There are many people who your network shouldn't be without. Do you have to have them all on your list now? No. Should you be working to include them? Definitely!

The best time to build your network is before you need it: before your car is 10 years old and in need of frequent repair, before a parent is ready to go into a nursing home, before you need a reference, and before someone close to you dies.

Networking Notes

- Dig deep into your expanded network and see what you find. There probably are many contacts you haven't considered yet.
- Don't overlook categories such as the parents of your children's friends, younger siblings of your friends, and former teachers. These people—and their connections—might be valuable additions to your network.
- Identify people you might need to know for one reason or another: doctors, lawyers, auto mechanics, electricians, and plumbers.
- Try to get people in your network before you actually need them.

CHAPTER | 8

DETERMINE WHAT YOU NEED FROM PROSPECTIVE MEMBERS OF YOUR NETWORK

If the title of this chapter made you pause and the word "exploitation" popped into your head, good for you! You've exhibited a high degree of sensitivity to one of the biggest networking no-nos: taking advantage of a relationship.

Some people—probably many people—still think of networking as a shameless, hard-sell approach to marketing yourself. You know, the salesman in the bad suit who just won't leave you alone when you're trying to eat your lunch, or the unsolicited photographer who took that cute picture of your daughter at the carnival and now calls you three times a week to set up a studio session. Well, these guys aren't networkers. They're pushy, unprofessional professionals who will put themselves out of business if they don't change the way they operate.

Having said all that, try to push the "e" word (exploitation) right back out of your head. Real networkers, like the one you're learning to be, aren't pushy or obnoxious. They fully understand that networking is a two-way street, and they use it to help others as well as to get help. So, don't be put off when you're asked to identify how Jane, a banker on your list, can help you. Hopefully, Jane is looking over her list right about now, figuring out how you can help her.

F.Y.I.

Did you ever get a salesperson on the phone who just wouldn't quit? Not too long ago, I got a call on a Saturday morning from a guy selling magazine subscriptions. I told him no thanks. This guy just wouldn't quit. He hounded and insisted and was generally obnoxious.

You know what? I ordered a magazine, just to get rid of him. I was furious. When the invoice came, I not only canceled it but also sent a letter to the company, explaining what had happened and how disgusted I was.

WHAT CAN WHO DO, AND WHAT CAN WHO DO FOR YOU?

That heading may sound like the title of a Dr. Seuss book, but it's really an important question.

As you meet new people, make new contacts, and expand your networking list, you'll become better and better prepared to handle problems that come along. The trick is knowing exactly who can do what for you, then knowing how to approach that person for help. When you have targeted the strengths of each person on your list, you will be prepared to make fast, direct contact when a need arises.

Have you lost your job as a victim of downsizing? It's not an ideal situation, but you'll be confident about finding a new job knowing that folks on your networking list can help you out. Are you feeling sick? That's a problem, but somebody surely can recommend a top-notch doctor. Need a special gift for an important client on short notice? Call your contact over at the gift shop, who'll choose something, wrap it beautifully, and have it delivered A.S.A.P.

Think about your networking list. There's your networking core, then the expanded network. Each person on your list is capable doing something for you; let's try to clarify exactly what it is that each person offers.

A WORD TO THE WISE

One of the greatest benefits of effective networking is that it gives you peace of mind. If something comes up, you've got people you can depend on. Networking is as complex as corporate mergers and takeovers, and as simple as having a bunch of friends to call on if you should suddenly need a babysitter or a ride to work.

Your Core Group

Even as a kid, you probably networked within your family. You didn't call it networking then; it was just trying to get what you wanted. Did you and your brother ever work a deal where he'd mow the grass on Saturday because you wanted to go to the ball game, but you'd have to take out the trash for four weeks straight? You approached your brother for help, and you got what you wanted. Then your brother, knowing he had some leverage, immediately networked back and got you to do something for him. Kid stuff? Sure. But it worked!

If you've maintained a good relationship with your family, they still can be your best networking sources. Even if the members of your immediate and close extended family aren't particularly powerful, knowledgeable, educated, or well connected, they know one thing very well: you. They know what motivates you and what makes you discouraged. They know your history, your quirks, and your strengths and can help, accordingly.

Your family and your close friends also are excellent networking sources because they care about you more than anybody else does. Let's face it—they're willing to do a lot more for you than some guy you met four years ago on the train to Chicago. If you're lucky enough to be part of a close family and have good friends, count your blessings and start networking.

Coworkers

Coworkers are good networking sources for several reasons. You spend a lot of time together, which gives you ample opportunity to discover ways in which you can help one another. Also, you have similar work-related interests, goals, and—presumably—incentive to achieve those goals.

Don't make the mistake of restricting your networking efforts with coworkers to work-related matters. Remember that people have lives outside of work, too, in which they use and share talents and interests you might not even know about. Some ways that coworkers can help each other include the following:

- **Warning a fellow employee that something is about to happen in the workplace that affects him or her.** If you learn that another round of layoffs is coming that will affect the accounting department, give your buddy in accounting some advance notice so he can get a head start on his job search.
- **Working together on talks, presentations, and projects.** If you know that your office mate has to finish laying out the annual report before she leaves for the day, offer to proofread it for her. It will make her job easier, and she'll owe you one.
- **Taking a new employee under your wing and showing him or her the ropes.** Remember how it feels to be the new kid on the block? This is one of the nicest things you can do for a new employee, and it will be remembered.
- **Offering support and encouragement when times get bad.** Nearly everyone who works experiences occasional discouragement or frustration on the job. Being there for a coworker who is having a bad day is a much-appreciated show of support.

BE CAREFUL!

For whatever reasons, coworkers tend to fall prey to the nasty business of gossip and innuendo. Telling secrets might be a form of networking but certainly not a positive or useful form. Being labeled as a gossip or a back-stabber isn't going to advance your networking efforts one bit.

People in Your Groups or Clubs

As a member of groups or clubs, you'll meet a wide variety of people with experience, knowledge, and expertise in many fields. They'll know other interesting people that you don't know, thus giving you an opportunity to expand your network even further.

Whether you belong to a quilting bee, a professional society, or a church choir, get to know the backgrounds of other members, and keep your eyes open for opportunities to network.

Your Extended Network

Your extended network includes a lot of people. People you know well, acquaintances you don't know well, and others about whom you know very little. Identifying what these people can do can be difficult. You'll have to be ready to do a little research to learn the strengths and areas of expertise of all the people on your networking list.

If you don't know much about a person with whom you hope to network, ask somebody who knows. If the person is prominent in the community or in the public eye, look through back issues of newspapers to find out what's been written and check out the Who's Who directory. Be creative.

When I worked for a newspaper, I could find out a person's address, phone number, and occupation just by looking in a city or county directory that was shelved in the public library. Maybe you should check out your library. If you know where the person works, search the Internet for the company's Web site or a personal Web page.

Your Family's Families and Friends

Your family might have family and friends all over the place, many of whom could be extremely useful and valuable members of your network, but you don't know them very well. Fortunately, these potential networking sources come with a built-in means of accessibility and information—your family.

Say, for example, that you know your sister-in-law's brother is a financial advisor in New York City. You've only met Ed twice, and you always get him confused with his brother Ben, the lawyer. You don't feel comfortable calling Ed, but you've got a good friend who's dying for an informational interview with a financial advisor. You also happen to owe this friend a big favor. You're not sure whether Ed would be willing or able to help you, but you figure it's worth a shot. After all, you are related—indirectly. Because you're not comfortable calling Ed directly, do the logical thing and call your sister-in-law. Maybe your friend will make a connection, maybe not, but you have to exhaust your options.

If your father's best friend and golf buddy just retired as accounting manager of the XYZ Company, and you're looking for a job as an accountant, which of these options would you choose?

1. Send a résumé to the XYZ Company with a cover letter asking to be notified if any positions should happen to become available.

2. Ask your dad to mention to his friend that you'll be calling him to see if he might have any information concerning the employment situation at XYZ.

If you chose option 1, go back to the beginning of the book and start again. If you chose option 2, then you're starting to get a feel for the power of networking.

Your Friends' Families and Friends

Your friends' families and friends are great possibilities for networking contacts. If you need to find out about them so you know how they'll best fit into your networking efforts, your friends are the obvious source of information. Most people like to talk about other people they know.

For a long time, I'd known that the sister and brother-in-law of a friend of mine were restoring a log cabin. My friend mentioned it every now and then, but it was never a lengthy topic of conversation, and I really didn't know much about it. Then, one day, my brother called and told me he'd just bought an old log cabin. He wanted to fix it up and eventually make it into a summer home. Did I know anybody who knew anything about log cabins? Although I had very little information at that time, I knew where to get it. My friend hooked up her sister and brother-in-law with my brother. Over the next couple of years, the owners of the two log cabins shared a lot of information—the best places to get materials, who the best contractors were, and lots more about log cabin renovation and preservation.

Families of Your Kids' Friends

If your child's school publishes a directory that lists the names, addresses, phone numbers, and occupations of each kid's parents, consider it a gold mine of information. You have a great networking tool in that directory.

Even if you don't get a directory, there are ways to find out who's doing what. Get an idea of which parents make things happen in school, for example, who runs the committees and organizes public events. These are the people that you should meet.

Which parents were in the classrooms on career day, and what did they talk about? If one child's mom is a lawyer and you think she'd be a perfect addition to your "Citizens to Stop the Toxic Waste Burner" group, pick up the phone and ask her. You and she have a natural connection: your kids.

Your Spouse's Friends and Coworkers

Ask your spouse for help on this one. Be careful—this situation can get a bit tricky sometimes. For instance, my husband is happy to tell me how his friends and coworkers might be of help to me but doesn't like feeling responsible if I ask and come up empty. He also is sometimes reluctant to ask his friends for "extras." I know he doesn't mind sharing his network, but he doesn't like to feel that he's let me down if I don't make a connection. Still, there's no reason to look elsewhere when you've got a perfectly good network sharing your home.

People You Work with but Don't Know Very Well

Unless you haven't gotten to know these people because you don't care to know them, start getting acquainted. You'll never know what someone can add to your network if you never give them a chance.

Former Colleagues

A busy schedule or a new job is no reason not to keep up with people you used to work with. These contacts are in the workplace, they know you and your skills, and they can be very valuable to you if you should find yourself back in the job market.

It's sometimes difficult to forget hard feelings toward former colleagues if you weren't on the best of terms when you parted company. If that's the case, you have to overcome those feelings, because you never know when your paths might cross again.

Don't make new relationships at the expense of old ones. Remember that Girl Scout song? "Make new friends, but keep the old / One is silver and the other's gold."

I'D LIKE YOU TO MEET...

Susan Larson Williams, vice president for human resources at VF Corporation, says her company recently lost the president of one of its major divisions to a competitor. The former president left behind a lot of hard feelings because people felt that he had betrayed them.

Susan worked hard to get over any bad feelings about the ex-president because she knows that someday she might need him. "This is a young, smart guy who's going to be in the apparel industry for a long time," she said. "I was upset when he left, like everyone was. But I don't believe in burning bridges. If I would lose my job in five years, I might need to know this guy."

Other Members of the Boards or Committees on Which You Serve

This is an important group of networking contacts. Those who serve on boards and committees are often high-profile people who know a lot of other people. They're very valuable for you to know because of that.

All your relationships should be cultivated, but these relationships should be nurtured. Volunteer to help with some community projects, and get to know some of your municipal officials. If you live in a northern state, establishing and keeping up a relationship with the head of your township's streets department may pay off for many a winter to come. After all, who do you think maps out the routes for the snow plows?

People You Meet at Social Events

Part of the beauty of social events is that you never know who will be there. You might completely unexpectedly get a chance to meet someone you've always wanted to but thought you never would. If that happens, you'd better be ready.

Say you meet the president—the head honcho—of the XYZ Company at your cousin's wedding. It turns out that this man is an old school chum of the groom's dad and he's known your cousin's new husband since he was born. Three don'ts apply to this situation:

1. Don't—I'll repeat, *don't*—sidle up to the guy with a résumé in your hand.
2. Don't even sidle up to him with a business card in your hand.
3. Don't lose the opportunity to make an impression.

How do you make an impression without a résumé or business card? Introduce yourself and give a little bit of background (we'll learn more about making dynamite first impressions in Chapter 10). Be gracious, and keep your conversation short. Do, however, ask if you might give him a brief call on Monday, perhaps to get the name of someone you could talk to about opportunities within the accounting field and at the XYZ Company, in particular.

If done properly, you can pull this off. Don't be a pest, but don't let an opportunity go by. If you do miss your chance, don't feel too bad. At least you know you've got a connection with this guy: your cousin and her new husband.

Members of Your Place of Worship

There definitely are people in your place of worship who will be valuable to your network, but you have to be careful. If other members get the impression that you joined the congregation or volunteered to serve on a committee for the primary purpose of meeting people who can be of benefit to you, look out. You're liable to see people move to another seat when you sit down next to them.

That's not to say that networking doesn't occur in such places. It does, all the time. In fact, it's encouraged. Does your place of worship hold a coffee fellowship before or after the service? Pot-luck dinners? Picnics? These gatherings, intended for members to get to know each other better, are natural and perfectly acceptable opportunities for networking.

So go ahead and find out as much as you can about your fellow worshippers. Use the member directory to put names to faces and get phone numbers. You'll find plenty of people with whom you'll want to network. Just do so at the appropriate times.

Professionals and Businesspeople

On the surface, it's pretty obvious what a professional person can do for you. A lawyer (a good one, anyway) can help when you find yourself in a bit of legal trouble. A doctor can make you feel better (hopefully) when you're sick. An accountant can (maybe) find some tax advantages you hadn't thought of, or at least keep the IRS from knocking at your door.

Look beyond the obvious to see what else lawyers, doctors, and accountants can do for you. These professional types usually are well-known, generally respected, and well-connected people in the community. One in your corner sure can't hurt if you ever need some information or a connection.

The same goes for the business people you deal with. Sure, you get good service from the couple at the corner store, know a guy who does a great job repairing your shoes, and can get a great price on a late-model car from your buddy at the dealership. Those people also know a lot of people, too, and a lot about what's going on around town. It is to your advantage to get to know them better.

Neighbors

What's the best way to find out what your neighbors can contribute to your network? Get to know them. Too many of us live in neighborhoods where we know our neighbors only by the cars we see pulling into the garages every night. What's the point of having neighbors if you never see them?

Plan a get-together—it doesn't have to be anything elaborate—a cocktail party or a back-yard picnic with hamburgers and hot dogs is perfect. Any occasion that allows people to talk and get to know each other in a relaxed setting will be perfect. A neighbor is a terrible thing to waste!

Teachers, Professors, and Instructors

Teachers have credibility. If a teacher says you're smart, people will believe that you're smart. If your mom says you're smart, well—so what? Use your present and former teachers, professors, and instructors for references whenever applicable, and don't overlook them as connections to other people for your network.

A WORD TO THE WISE

When you have a problem or a need, first look within your network for someone to help you. If you come up empty-handed, then look for someone within your network to help you locate someone outside of your network who can.

WHAT IF NOBODY CAN HELP?

You may find yourself someday without a contact who can help you with a particular problem. If you're used to being able to pick up the phone and find out whatever you want to know, this can be a frustrating and upsetting experience.

Say, for instance, that your wife has just been diagnosed with chronic fatigue syndrome. The doctors she's seen haven't been particularly sympathetic, and they don't seem to know too much about this little-known condition. You figure you have to find a new doctor—fast. You're determined to find the best physician available, so you plug into your network. Someone must have a lead. You make calls, but to no avail. Nobody knows anything about chronic fatigue syndrome, nor has anyone heard about doctors who treat it. You feel helpless and can't understand why your network has failed you.

Your network hasn't failed you; you just haven't worked hard enough. You're going to have to expand your network until it includes someone who can give you the information you need. Rack your brain and try to think of any connections. Then, pick up the phone and try again. Press a little harder. Dig a little deeper.

Okay, your contacts don't know any doctors who specialize in chronic fatigue syndrome. Do they know of anyone who has had the disease, or of somebody who knows someone who's had it? Does anyone have a contact who might have researched the disease and its treatment? Does anybody know a good doctor who might be able to give a referral? Information you need doesn't have to come from your existing contacts, just through them.

A SCIENCE OR AN ART?

You've spent a whole chapter learning how to determine what people can do for you and how they fit into your network. Don't be put off by all this categorizing and departmentalizing we've been doing. Networking requires organization and planning, but once everything is in place, you'll find out that it's a fun and natural process that even allows a little creativity to keep it working well.

Networking Notes

- Figuring out what each person on your networking list has to offer doesn't mean you're exploiting or taking advantage of anyone. Networks are designed so that all members will give—and get—help.
- Target the strengths and abilities of each person on your network so that you know exactly who to contact when a particular need arises. Encourage members of your network to do the same with you.
- If you can't find a member of your network to help you with a particular problem, dig deeper. Look for someone on your networking list who might know someone else who can help.
- Everyone can help in some way—don't overlook any member of your network when identifying strengths and abilities.
- Don't take advantage of any member of your network by asking for help at an inappropriate time or in an inappropriate manner.
- All the preparation involved with starting a network can be overwhelming. Don't become discouraged. After you get your network organized, networking will be like a second nature.

CHAPTER | 9

DON'T OVERLOOK THE NETWORK YOU DON'T REALIZE YOU HAVE

Remember Joe, from junior high school? He always wore that red and white striped shirt, and he brought peanut butter and jelly sandwiches for lunch every day for three years. He was really smart but never acted like he was. He loved to fish for sunnies down in the little creek near your house and used corn for bait. And he knew that great shortcut through the field, so you could get from his house to yours in just under 10 minutes.

Maybe you remember Joe, maybe you don't. After all, you haven't seen him since junior high school, and we don't even want to think about how long ago that was. It's funny, though. Now that you're thinking about it... didn't your mom just mention that she ran into Joe's mom in the grocery store? Joe's mom told your mom that Joe had moved to Charlotte, North Carolina, after he graduated from Duke University. He had opened his own accounting firm and was doing really well.

You know, Joe would be a great person to have in your network. Guess what? He's already in. How can a guy be part of your network when you haven't seen him since junior high? I know, it's a little bit of a stretch. Well, you know Joe, and he knows you. At least he will remember you after you reestablish contact. So, what do you do? You call Joe, that's what.

If you think you can't call Joe because you haven't talked to him in 12 years, think again. Wouldn't you be glad to hear from Joe if he called you? Sure, you might think it's a little funny to suddenly get a phone call from a guy who you haven't seen since you were wearing Health-tex jeans, but you'd be glad to hear from him, right? If you tell yourself you can't call Joe because it's inappropriate, pushy, or presumptuous, then you're talking yourself out of a chance for some great networking.

A WORD TO THE WISE

Sometimes your best networking contacts are just out of sight, around the corner. These people have gotten away, but you can easily bring them back into your network.

IT'S QUIZ TIME!

Let's take a minute here to evaluate your networking graces. Read the following three openers, then choose the example that you think would best reestablish your ties with Joe and make him eager to be included in your network.

Finding The Right Words

You just got Joe's phone number from his mom, and Joe has just come on the line.

1. ___ "Hello, Joe? My name is Mike Madison. I'm sure you don't remember me because I haven't talked to you for 12 years, but my mom ran into your mom in the grocery store, and your mom said you've got your own business and are doing great, so I thought I'd give you a call."

2. ___ "Hello, Joe? This is Mike Madison calling. (Pause and wait for a response.) Yeah, Mike Madison from Browntown, that's right! How are you doing? I've been thinking about you a lot the last couple of weeks and thought I'd give you a call to try to catch up a little bit. It's been a long time, hasn't it?"

3. ___ "Hi Joe. It's Mike Madison. How've you been? I was thinking that maybe the next time you're in town to visit your folks, you and I could get together for a golf game or something. I'd like to talk with you about a few things. Or, I might be able to drop by and see you when I get into North Carolina. I bring the family down to the Outer Banks every summer."

Well, which one did you pick? If you chose opener 1 or opener 3, then you'll have to start paying closer attention. The correct answer is opener 2. Here's why: In opener 1, Mike was rambling and juvenile sounding, but at least he could still pass for a nice guy. In opener 3, Mike was arrogant. In opener 2, however, Mike sounded sincere and caring—the kind of guy anyone would be happy to network with.

Opener 1: Nay

The first conversation (or Mike's side to the conversation) has some major problems.

- The greeting is rambling and unfocused.
- Mike assumes that Joe doesn't remember him, which indicates that Mike doesn't feel that he's a memorable kind of guy.
- Mike establishes distance between himself and Joe when he says he hasn't talked to Joe for 12 years.
- Referring to "my mom" and "your mom" makes Mike sound like he's 14 years old.
- Telling Joe that he's calling because he heard Joe's been very successful makes Mike appear opportunistic, as if he wants something.

Opener 2: Yea

This definitely is the best of the three examples.

- Mike draws Joe into the conversation right away by waiting for a response.
- Mike doesn't assume Joe won't remember him, but he's not pushy either.
- Referring to their hometown, Mike emphasizes their shared history.
- By asking how Joe is doing, Mike indicates that he's interested in Joe's life.
- Mike establishes himself as someone who cares about Joe by telling him he's been thinking about him lately.

- By saying, "It's been a long time, hasn't it?" Mike again establishes a common history by referring to a shared past.

Opener 3: Big Nay

This example is arguably the worst of the three.

- Mike assumes that Joe remembers him.
- Mike presumes that he can pick up where their friendship left off without reestablishing communication.
- Because he never asks Joe how he's doing, Mike comes off as being very self-absorbed; the conversation is all about Mike.
- Mike takes for granted that Joe would even be interested in meeting him for a quick cup of coffee, much less spend an afternoon playing golf with him.
- Instead of offering to make a special point to see him, Mike puts down Joe by saying he could "drop by" on his way to the Outer Banks.

REESTABLISHING LOST FRIENDSHIPS

All this discussion about Joe and Mike, their moms, and the grocery store is meant to make you more aware of the network you might not realize you have. If there's one Joe out there, chances are there are more people like him. So, what about Joe?

By calling Joe, Mike took the first step in reestablishing regular contact. Then what? If Mike is smart and network savvy (as in opener 2), he'll use his first conversation with Joe to just get reacquainted. He won't ask Joe for a thing—he'll simply catch up on what's been happening for the past 12 years. They'll tell each other about college, jobs, and families. They'll reminisce a bit about the old days and remember that cranky teacher they had for math in eighth grade. Mike can bring Joe up to date on some of the people he still sees but with whom Joe has lost touch and tell Joe the latest hometown news.

After they've chatted for a while, Mike will wrap up the conversation before either of them runs out of things to talk about. He will, by all means, ask Joe if it's okay to call him again soon and offer Joe his phone number. He'll also say something like, "I'm so glad we're back in touch, Joe. I've thought about you a lot over the years, and I've always hoped everything was going well for you."

When Joe and Mike finish their call, several things should have been accomplished:

1. Mike and Joe have rekindled their friendship.
2. Mike has established himself as Joe's contemporary and has made it clear that he's no longer the kid Joe remembers.
3. Their shared history has been firmly established and is used as the starting point for a new relationship.
4. They've made plans to stay in touch.

Keeping in Touch

Once contact has been reestablished, it's Mike's job to make sure it continues. Joe very well might make it easy for Mike by calling the following week to touch base. As with any networking initiative, Mike should follow up the initial phone call with a note to Joe. The note could say something like, "It was really great to catch up with you yesterday, Joe. I'm glad everything's going so well for you, both personally and professionally. I'm looking forward to staying in touch with you, and I hope to see you the next time you and your family are in town. I'd love to hear more about starting a business from scratch, as I might someday be in a position to do the same thing." In his note, Mike should acknowledge interest in Joe's personal and professional lives and set the stage to get to know more about both.

If Mike doesn't hear from Joe, he should wait for a couple of weeks, then call again. He should be friendly and interested in how things are going. He also needs to remember that he and Joe are still getting reacquainted. This isn't the time to start pumping Joe for information about starting a business or about anything else.

Do What Comes Naturally

Hopefully, Mike and Joe's relationship will continue to grow. They'll play a round of golf the next time Joe comes to town. The time after that, they'll go out to dinner with their wives. The next time, Joe and his wife will bring their two-year-old daughter for a picnic at Mike's house. Mike will put Joe back in touch with a couple of the other guys they used to fish with. Pretty soon, Joe will be firmly established as a member of Mike's network, and Mike will be a part of Joe's. At that point, Mike can set up a time to call Joe and pick his brains about starting his own business, and Joe will be more than happy to help him.

Mike and Joe are two lucky guys. In addition to expanding their networks, they've regained a valuable friendship. Like any relationship, it will require maintenance. They'll be willing to tend to it because they both stand to benefit greatly.

Who's just around your corner? Take a few minutes to think about who might be around your corner—people you haven't seen for a long time, who used to be close friends, who you have lost touch with, or who you have not kept up with. We all have let some relationships wither. With focused energy and care, however, we might be able to bring them back to life.

Explore Every Possible Connection

Sometimes we overlook connections because we've lost sight of them, like Mike did with Joe. Other times, we overlook connections because we assume the person in question wouldn't be willing to help. Still other times, though, we overlook connections just because we don't acknowledge a person as networking partner. To us, the person is just a friend, someone's mom, a friend's brother, or an old teacher.

When we rule out possible connections as real connections, we risk missing out on some good opportunities.

DON'T "PSYCH" YOURSELF OUT

Sometimes you might overlook a connection because you think that person won't be willing to help or network with you, but you have nothing to lose—all you have to do is ask.

As part of a writing project I once had, I interviewed the owners or principals of 50 businesses in my county. The businesses ranged from small shops to huge corporations. It was a great project, because I got to meet 50 well-connected, influential people in my community. It also gave me 50 chances to practice some networking skills. You can be sure that I followed each interview with a note, thanking the officer for the meeting, and then added each name to my files. I also sent copies of the articles I wrote about each company to the appropriate person so they could see what I had written before it appeared in the book.

About two months after I completed the project, I needed a letter of reference to send along with a job application. I really wanted to ask the president of one of the major corporations I had written about, but I wasn't sure that he would agree to do it. I thought it might seem presumptuous of me to ask him, because I had met him only once. After agonizing over this for a few days, I figured I had nothing to lose by asking and called him.

I'D LIKE YOU TO MEET...

Chris Flynn, an independent mortgage broker, found networking contacts just around his corner a couple of years ago. At a dinner sponsored by a community group, he ran into a woman who had been a babysitter for Chris and his four siblings when they were kids. Chris hadn't seen her for years because she had moved from Pennsylvania to Illinois. They had great fun catching up and reminiscing.

During the course of their conversation, Chris discovered that they shared a common interest and concern about a church they had both attended when Chris was a kid. St. Mary Magdelene's church in LaAnna, Pennsylvania, had long been used by a parish of the Catholic Diocese of Scranton. A new, bigger church had been built, so St. Mary Magdelene's had been standing vacant and unattended for eight years. It had deteriorated badly, and Chris and his former babysitter were among those who were deeply concerned.

Their conversation that night was the incentive they needed to take action. They started some heavy-duty networking to save the church. A letter-writing campaign, starting with the bishop of the diocese and working down, enlisted support and resulted in pledges to help save the church. It also so happened that the son of Bill Giles (owner of the Philadelphia Phillies) had been married in the church, so the "save the church" group was able to get some help from Giles, too.

Before long, the outcry to "save the church" was so great that the pastor responsible for the building had no choice but to help fund the repair project out of his budget. Renovations began, and the church is now in good condition again.

Chris teamed up with a woman he hadn't seen for close to 30 years to do something good in his community. You can bet that they are now firmly entrenched in each other's networks.

To my delight, he said he'd be happy to write the letter. He had liked the article and thanked me for sending it. In the recommendation, he not only praised my writing but said I was professional and thoughtful, as well. This man turned out to be a great connection, even though I had almost convinced myself that there was no connection at all. I almost overlooked a good opportunity by failing to recognize this man as a contact.

You'll learn more about dealing with rejection in the next chapter, but suffice to say that it will happen. Not every company president is going to be willing to write a letter of recommendation for you. When rejection comes your way, simply say, "Thank you anyway," pick yourself up, and move on.

A WORD TO THE WISE

If you don't ask, you'll never know whether a person would be willing to help you out or be part of your network.

Keep Your Eyes and Ears Open

I know a woman who worked in the admissions office of a college in New York. As an admissions counselor, Patty processed applications and screened potential students. She was working on her master's degree at the same time, and her plan was to spend a couple of years there, then move to a bigger college while she pursued a doctorate degree. Eventually, she hoped to be pretty high on the food chain of college administrators at a decent-sized school. Her plan took an unexpected twist, however, that was directly related to her networking.

While working in the admissions office, Patty got to know the dean of the college of arts and sciences. His office was in the same building, and he often would stop by the admissions office to say hello. He had been at the college for years and was very near to retiring. He knew everybody and was very friendly.

Patty became very fond of this man. She said he reminded her of her grandfather, who had died years before. They got to be good friends. He introduced Patty to his wife, and they started inviting Patty for dinner. Soon, the dean and his wife had become a surrogate family to Patty, whose own family lived quite far away.

After Patty had been an admissions counselor for about a year and a half, the director of admissions announced he was leaving. A search for a new director began, and the dean encouraged Patty to apply for it. Patty tossed her hat into the ring, with little hope of success. Several people in the admissions office had been there longer and held positions higher than hers. She figured that if the job were to be given to someone already working at the college, it certainly would be one of them.

One month after she applied, Patty learned to her great surprise that she was one of three people being considered for the director's job. She went through the interviewing process and eventually was offered the position, which she accepted.

It was a great opportunity for her, and she stayed there for five years before moving to a larger school.

Until several years later, Patty had no idea that the reason she got the director's job was because her friend the dean had lobbied hard for her. This man was well respected in the college community, and his endorsement carried a lot of weight. Fortunately, he thought well enough of Patty to lobby unsolicited on her behalf. Had he needed some prodding, Patty would have been out of luck, because it would never have occurred to her to ask.

Patty thought of the dean and his wife as close friends, almost family—not contacts or networking partners. It never had occurred to her that the friendship would be so valuable professionally. Later, she said she would have felt like she was taking advantage of a friendship to ask the dean to intervene on her behalf, but she's very glad that he did. "Looking back on it, that was one of the most significant points of my career," Patty explains. "It allowed me to advance much faster than I would have otherwise. I'll always be grateful to my friend for helping me."

By the way, Patty has moved on to a larger college, earned her Ph.D., and is in line to become a vice president.

Who Else Is Waiting To Help?

The people we overlook as potential networking partners very well may be the ones who are most willing. Family members and close friends generally want to help, but we often miss chances because we don't think of our families and friends as being in a position to help. I mean, how can your mom help you find a job? She's your mom, not a networking partner.

Think about this for a minute. Your mom is one of your greatest advocates, just because she's your mom. She'll go to bat for you because she wants you to succeed. If you succeed, you'll be happy, and she wants you to be happy. How can she help? Who does she know?

If your mom is anything like mine, she knows just about everybody. She knows the owners and former owners of established businesses because she either went to school with them or has been doing business with them for years. She knows everybody at the grocery store, from the manager to the stock boys, and is particularly friendly with the guy in the seafood department. She always knows what's going on around town because her hairdresser keeps her informed; what she misses at the beauty salon, she catches up with at bridge club or garden club.

My mom has friends from when she was PTA president and from church, the swim club, her schools, my father's schools, and her children's schools. She keeps in touch with some of her children's friends and some of her friends' children. My mom knows a lot of people and on more than one occasion has used her connections to get jobs for my brother and sisters and me. I'd never overlook my mom as a connection, and you shouldn't either.

Maybe your mom isn't the one who knows everyone. It could be your dad, your minister, your best friend's brother, or your grandmother's friend. Whoever it is, be sure that you don't overlook the connections that you might realize you have. Think about all the people you meet in a day: your kid's teacher, people who clean your windows, roofers, the elderly woman who lives down the street, a teenager who sold you candy for a school fundraiser. Who do they know? Carefully consider the possibility that these people are potential members of your network.

Never assume that someone has nothing to offer, because nearly everyone does. Your friends and family, although most overlooked, might be some of your best connections. And your new connections may become some of your best friends.

Ain't networking grand!

Networking Notes

- Sometimes our best contacts are the ones we overlook.
- When reestablishing contact with someone you haven't seen for a while, make the initial contact, keep in touch, and let the relationship develop naturally.
- Even relationships that have been neglected can be brought back to life with some effort.
- Networking skills that can be used to your advantage are worth their weight in gold.
- Networking skills that are used to promote something good in your community are worth twice their weight in gold.
- Never assume that someone can't or won't help you; you'll never know unless you ask.
- The people closest to you generally are your best advocates.
- Take another look at people you see every day and consider them as possible networking contacts.
- It's great when friends become networking partners, but it's even better when networking partners become friends.

CHAPTER | 10

HOW TO CONVINCE SOMEONE TO NETWORK WITH YOU

Those of you who have just broken out in a cold sweat, relax! This exercise won't be hard at all. Take another quiz to see how well prepared you are to convince someone to network with you.

IT'S QUIZ TIME!

Circle what you believe to be the correct answer—true or false—for each statement.

1. Most people I approach will be too busy to help and might even resent the fact that I asked. True / False
2. People probably will help someone they know but not someone they don't know. True / False
3. It's not a good idea to ask someone you don't know to help you. True / False

4. When I do contact someone, I should introduce myself and then wait for them to offer to help me. True / False

5. The way that I introduce myself is very important and could affect the person's willingness to help me. True / False

6. I should prepare an introduction for myself before I meet someone with whom I want to network. True / False

7. My introduction should include specific information that will be useful to the person I'm meeting. True / False

8. I should tell the person I'm meeting exactly what I want. True / False

9. Given the choice, meeting someone in person is better than a phone call. True / False

10. Because this first meeting isn't really an interview, I can be casual about my dress and appearance. True / False

If you chose "True" for statements 5 through 9 and "False" for everything else, you're already a pro! If you got some answers wrong, that's okay. You'll learn everything you need to know as you go along. There's lots of good information to help everyone here.

> ### I'D LIKE YOU TO MEET...
>
> Karen Kelly is a busy editorial director at a New York City publishing firm, but she is happy to make time for someone who asks for help. "I like to help people," she says. "I love to give advice, for whatever it's worth."

OVERCOMING FEAR OF MEETING PEOPLE

Many people lose great opportunities for networking because they can't bring themselves to approach someone they don't know and initiate a conversation. Lots of people even have trouble making a phone call to someone they don't know. They feel that it's intrusive and assuming to think that the person will take time to help them.

If you answered "True" to statement 1, you're probably one of those people. But you're wrong. Most people are happy to help people, even if they don't know them. "Most people like to help other people," says Susan Larson Williams. "It makes them feel good to be able to do something for somebody else."

Some networking experts take this thought a bit further and claim that you're doing your contact a favor when you ask for referrals or contacts. The logic is that when you tell your contact that you're looking for contacts because you're job hunting, you've given something of value: information. He or she then knows that you're looking for a job and that you need contacts and/or referrals.

Personally, I think the second explanation is a bit far-fetched. Tell yourself that you'll have opportunities to do that person favors later on. Meanwhile, assume that he or she would be happy to help you because most people like to help others.

Don't be naive and think that someone who has never met you will be willing to do as much for you as a friend or family member. It would be very surprising if your new contact not only gave you some referrals but also asked you out to dinner that night and offered you a job the next day. In fact, I'd seriously wonder whether a contact willing to do so much for you might have an ulterior motive.

Remember that asking friends and family for help is a perfectly acceptable and smart first step. If we all had well-connected family and friends, we'd never have to approach strangers for help. When you do, don't hesitate. Make a plan, practice your lines a few times, and pick up the phone. Better yet, march into your future networking partner's office (after having made an appointment, of course), give your best smile and a firm handshake, and start your pitch.

In an interview with Hal Lancaster of the *Wall Street Journal*, networking guru Harvey Mackay said that experienced professionals are willing to help younger people with less experience but often don't get asked. "I think there are a lot of old fuds like myself who are willing to help, but people don't ask," Mackay says. "The three reasons people don't ask for help are rejection, rejection, rejection."

A WORD TO THE WISE

Re-read Susan Larson Williams' quote: "Most people like to help other people. It makes them feel good to be able to do something for somebody else." Read it again. Repeat it a couple of times to yourself. Now, say it out loud.

Make this quote your motto. It is much less intimidating to ask someone for help if you believe that he or she will welcome your request.

What If the Answer Is No?

Lest I paint too rosy a picture concerning this topic of asking strangers for help, you need to be aware that some people will sometimes say no. Some might even give you the cold shoulder. Expect the occasional call from a secretary, who tells you that the person you wanted to speak with really has nothing to offer you and has an extremely full schedule, anyway. You might even run into someone who is downright testy about your request.

F.Y.I.

Rejection doesn't happen to only novice networkers. During the course of writing this book, I called the office of the president and CEO of a major corporation. I wanted to see whether I could interview him about how he uses networking.

I knew that it would be difficult to get to see this man, but I'd done some research on this corporation and had visited the company on several occasions. I took a chance that he might remember me and agree to give up 20 minutes of his time. His secretary, who did remember me, sounded surprised at the request but agreed to ask on my behalf. Not even a half an hour later, the corporation's spokeswoman called back to tell me the CEO couldn't possibly take the time, even for a short interview.

Okay, I didn't get my interview, but I didn't lose anything either. In fact, making the phone call reestablished my connection with the company, and both people I spoke to mentioned the work I had done there. Was I rejected? I sure was. Upset? Not a bit.

Don't Dwell on Rejection

When rejection comes your way—and believe me, it will—accept it as a fact of networking life and move on. If you think you were rejected because you didn't introduce yourself as well as you might have, then fine-tune your script. You'll improve both your introduction and your confidence for the next time. If you feel like you came on too strong, consider how you can tone down your presentation a bit.

Whatever the reason, don't beat yourself up! The person who rejected you might have been having a bad day, you may have called or arrived at a bad time, or that person just might be a genuinely unpleasant person. If rejection comes from someone you don't know and who doesn't know you, then it can't be personal. People can't really dislike you if they don't know you!

Occasional rejection should never stop you from actively networking and pursuing leads that may take you somewhere.

MAKING THE CONTACT

When the time comes to ask somebody to be part of your network, you must be ready. You have only one chance to make a first impression, so it should be as good as it can be.

Regardless of whether you'll be making your contact by phone or in person, you'll need to prepare ahead of time. After you've figured out what you want to say (that will be much clearer by the end of this chapter), ask a friend to act out the meeting with you. Pretend your friend is the person you'll be meeting and give your very best sales pitch. If you're surprised at the use of the words "sales pitch," don't be. When you network, you're selling yourself.

If you answered "True" to statement 6 of the quiz, you're absolutely correct. You should have a carefully thought-out introduction for yourself prepared before you dial the phone number of the person you plan to ask for help. The worst thing you can do is get on the phone and realize that you're completely unprepared. A busy professional doesn't have time to listen to you stammer as you try to figure out what to say.

When Your Contact Is By Telephone

If you're going to be making your contact over the phone, you won't have to worry about whether your left shoe is scuffed or whether your hair is sticking up in the spot it always does. You do, however, need an excellent introduction, top-notch phone skills, and a positive manner that expresses self-confidence.

The Introduction

Experts do not agree about how long it should take for you to introduce yourself. Some say no more than 25 seconds, but others feel it can go as long as two minutes. Some recommend that the introduction should be the same, whether delivered over the phone or in person. Others think it's okay to make a longer introduction in person but that phone introductions should be kept brief.

A couple of things, though, are certain: Nobody wants to hear your entire background starting when you left the sixth grade and went to a new school. Nobody wants to listen to you whine about how you were downsized, lost your job because your boss never liked you, or have been out of college for a year and haven't been able to find a job. Don't ruin your chances of getting help by alienating the person you want on your team. Be considerate, upbeat, and professional.

If you decide you want to keep your phone introduction down to 25 seconds, that's fine. But if you find yourself speaking at rocket speed to cram everything you want to say into that short time frame, forget about it. It's better to give an introduction that is a bit longer but intelligible. Talking too quickly makes you appear nervous and unpracticed.

What Should I Say?

If you answered "True" to statement 7, you're right again. Your introduction, whether given over the phone or in person, should include specific information. The function of introducing yourself is to bring your contact quickly up to speed on who you are, why you're calling, and why he or she should help you.

You do not need to say that your brother went to school with your contact's wife's second cousin's daughter. Nor do you need to say how happy you are to finally make a connection because you tried calling on six different occasions and couldn't get past the secretary. Here's what your introduction *should* include:

- **Who you are:** "Hello, Mr. Jones. This is Sharon Smith calling."
- **Who referred you:** "I got your name from Walt Williams, who suggested that I give you a call." (Make sure you have permission to use Walt Williams' name, and never indicate that you were referred by someone if you weren't.)
- **What you do:** "Mr. Jones, I've been a newspaper reporter for six years, and have enjoyed the work tremendously."
- **What you want to do:** "Our paper was recently acquired by a chain, and my job is being eliminated. I'd like to use this opportunity to move to a bigger paper."
- **What you want your contact to do:** "Mr. Jones, I understand you have a lot of contacts in the newspaper business, and I was wondering if you could give me the names of some editors that I could contact."

Don't Beat Around the Bush

Some people do fine with their introductions until they get to the part where they need to ask for help. Then, they freeze up. If you do that, you've made the phone call for nothing.

You didn't call to give this person a rundown on your life at this particular point in time; you called to ask for help. Furthermore, your contact doesn't think that you just called for a little chat. After you explain who you are and where you got his or her name, the radar tuned in: You're calling to ask for something. Don't

BE CAREFUL!

Susan Larson Williams, vice president for human resources at VF Corporation, talks to many people who are looking for jobs, information, referrals, or other help. One of the biggest turn-offs, she says, is when someone name drops and pretends to know a top person in the company in an attempt to improve their own status.

Susan recalls the case of a realtor who called to see whether VF Corporation could use his services in helping to relocate some of its employees. The realtor said that Mackey McDonald, president of VF Corporation, was his neighbor and had suggested that he call.

Because VF has a certain realtor it uses when necessary, Susan thought the call was odd. When she asked McDonald about it, she found he had never recommended that the realtor call. In fact, he and the realtor weren't even neighbors.

If someone suggests that you call, then by all means use the name, Susan recommends—it's an advantage to have been referred by a higher-up within the company. But don't take advantage, and don't lie. Lies, even "little white lies" (exaggerations) instantly destroy your credibility, along with your chances of getting any sort of help, never mind a job.

---

keep the person you're calling in suspense, and don't wait for an offer of help. If your contact doesn't know what you want, then he or she doesn't know what to offer.

If you make it through your introduction, then your contact has all the information he or she needs about you at the time—who you are, how you got his or her name, what you do, what you want to do, and how he or she can help you—and you probably did it in less than 30 seconds. All our conversations should be so short and to the point! Now, the ball is out of your court, and you wait for him or her to respond.

Ideally, your contact will suggest that you come in for a meeting the following day. Mr. Jones, for example, would put you in touch with a dozen important and influential newspaper editors with whom he just happens to be on a first-name basis. He also was best man for five of them and is godfather to half their children.

If that happens, get the champagne in the fridge. Things are looking good.

Realistically, though, your contact will say something like, "I'll have to think about this. Why don't I call you in a couple of days after I get together some names." Oh no! Now you're worried. Is your contact being truthful, or is this a brush-off? You don't want to let on that you're sweating, so say something like, "Sure. Listen, I really appreciate your time. Any names you could pass along would be very helpful to me."

Before you get off the phone, tell your contact that you know he or she is busy, so if it's okay, you'll call back in several days if you haven't received a return call by that time. If your contact is going to call you, make sure to leave your phone number. As soon as you hang up, write your contact a note, thanking him or her for the meeting and reminding him or her that you'll call to get the names if you don't hear back in the next few days. If you have a fax machine or access to one, provide the number and suggest faxing information to you if it's more convenient that way.

Face-to-Face Contact

For many people, face-to-face meetings are more difficult than phone conversations, but they can have a greater impact. It's usually better to meet someone in person than on the phone, but I must admit that quiz statement 9—"Given the choice, meeting someone in person is better than a phone call"—is something of a trick question. Generally, the answer would be "True." However, there are exceptions.

If you're extremely uncomfortable during a personal meeting—to the point where it's impossible for you to look the person to whom you're speaking in the eye—and infinitely more comfortable on the phone, then you're better off using the phone. Of course, you're going to have to get with the program if you expect to be a successful networker. (See Chapter 3 to review how to overcome shyness and lack of confidence.) You can't do all your networking over the phone.

Another exception in the face-to-face versus telephone contact debate would be if, for instance, you had tangled with poison ivy over the weekend. A rash covers your face, arms, and hands. You look and feel awful. Although you really want to make your appointment today, you know that you look horrible and that some people are afraid of catching poison ivy from people who have it. In this case, a call prior to the appointed time is in order. You can explain the situation and request that meeting on the phone instead of in person.

Normally, you should go for the face-to-face meeting whenever possible. It gives you a chance to make an impression by looking your contact in the eye and flashing your best smile. It lets your contact see the confidence in your walk and feel it in your handshake.

If you're nervous about a personal meeting, practice with a friend. You'll feel better if you've run through your part of the conversation a few times. Practice your introduction by saying it as you look in the mirror. Tape record it to hear how you sound. The more you practice, the more natural and confident you'll be with it.

After the Handshake

Your in-person introduction will be much the same in person as it was over the phone. If you want to make it a little longer, mention your education or a previous job or reveal a bit more about your plans and goals. Just be sure to include the basics from the phone introduction:

- who you are,
- who referred you,
- what you do,
- what you want to do, and
- what you want your contact to do.

When you're face to face with your contact, you have some advantages you don't have over the phone.

- **You can leave your business card.** Business cards are invaluable reminders. If your contact puts your card on the desk, it will serve as a reminder of your visit and what he or she agreed to do for you.
- **You can leave your résumé, if appropriate.** You've only come to ask for the names of people who might be connections in the industry, but if your contact asks for a copy of your résumé, so much the better! He or she may want to pass it on or simply refer to your vital information in conversations with a colleague.
- **If your contact promises to get back in touch with you in a couple of days with some names, you can leave a paper with spaces for names and phone numbers.** Make sure it includes your name, phone number, and fax number, if you have one. If your contact is meant to mail the paper back to you, include a self-addressed stamped envelope.

What You Wear Matters

Technically speaking, this meeting is not a job interview. So, does it matter what you wear? Check quiz statement 10 and see if you got it right. Of course it matters what you wear!

Networking with one person in order to get the names of other people is as important as the interviews you hope to get with those other people. In a perfect world, we'd all look past physical appearances to what's inside a person. We'd be impressed by personal qualities such as loyalty and kindness instead of designer suits and handbags. In this world, unfortunately, designer labels get people noticed. Until someone has an opportunity to really get to know you, impressions are based on how you look.

Your contact probably will never know you as anything more than a person who came by looking for some names. His or her only impression of you will be based on what happens during that visit, so you can see why it's so important to look your best. When you go to a contact's office to ask for help, you should dress the way you would for a job interview (see Chapter 1 for a review).

If you don't have any designer originals in your closet, don't fret. Lack of such items won't ruin your chances of successful networking as long as you look clean, neat, and put together. By that, I mean pay attention to the details. It would be a shame to match a brand-new suit that fits you perfectly with scuffed shoes, panty-hose with runs, or a stained or wrinkled shirt. Take the time to look at your outfit—the whole thing—the day before your interview, when you still have time to polish, run to the drug store, iron, or go to the one-hour dry cleaner.

And by the way, that ratty old purse or briefcase whose handles are falling off is better left at home.

🤝 I'D LIKE YOU TO MEET

Linda Smith, a corporate human resources administrator for a major retailer based in Reading, Pennsylvania, is in charge of hiring dozens of people every time her company opens a new store. Her job is to fill positions from buyers to managers, cashiers, and stock people.

In this kind of job, Linda interviews all kinds of people. She says she thought she'd seen it all, until the day a woman showed up for her interview with pink rollers in her hair. "It was just amazing," Linda says. "How do you interview somebody when you can't keep your eyes off her head?"

Needless to say, the woman wasn't hired.

DON'T TRY TO BE SOMETHING YOU'RE NOT

Follow the suggestions in this chapter and you should have no trouble convincing someone to network with you. There's one more piece of advice, though, and it's arguably more important than anything you've read so far: Be yourself.

If you try to act like someone or something you're not, either over the phone or in person, it will be very obvious. Relax, think about your accomplishments, and make a list of your 10 best qualities. Hey! You're a pretty neat person, after all. Be confident, and be yourself.

Networking Notes

- When you approach someone to ask for help, remember that most people are happy to give advice and share their knowledge with someone who is interested.
- If somebody refuses to help you, don't take it personally—that person probably has reasons for saying no that have nothing whatsoever to do with you. It doesn't pay to dwell on rejection; it happens to everyone sometime.
- Prepare carefully for your approach to ask someone for help, whether it be over the phone or in person.
- When you call or meet with someone to ask for help, ask for it. Don't waste your time (and your contact's) beating around the bush.
- If someone offers to call you back with some names or other information, be sure to leave your phone number. Ask whether it's okay for you to call if you don't hear anything in a few days.
- Remember that meeting someone in person is generally better than a phone call—unless there are special circumstances.
- Dress neatly to make a good impression on the person you're going to ask to be part of your network.
- Never try to act like someone or something that you're not.

CHAPTER | 11

BE AWARE OF ALL NETWORKING POSSIBILITIES

You've heard stories about waitresses being approached by customers who just happened to be big-shot movie producers and who asked—no, begged—them to be in upcoming films. And you probably heard about the girl who was just walking down the street, minding her own business, when the head of the biggest modeling agency in town approached her and told her she was sure to be the next Elle MacPherson.

Most of us aren't that lucky. We've got to make things happen, and we can do exactly that with good networking.

Networking guru Harvey Mackay refers often to the "six degrees of separation." This term refers to the theory that a chain of no more than six people links every person in the world to every other person. (It also was the title of a Broadway show and movie.) Think about that! Therefore, you know somebody who knows somebody who knows somebody who knows somebody who knows somebody who knows Margaret Thatcher. You've got a network to the former prime minister of England!

I know that this idea sounds pretty far-fetched and that Margaret Thatcher most likely is not part of your networking plans. But the point is, you never know. And you never know who knows who, do you? That's why you always have to keep your eyes, ears, and mind open to networking opportunities. To be a really effective networker, you have to do it all the time. It has to become a way of life. If you pass up one experience, you pass up a chance to meet somebody who could add significantly to your network—or who might become a good friend.

"The main thing about networking is to put yourself out there," says Karen Kelly, the New York editorial director of Daybreak Books. She credits much of her success in the publishing industry to networking. "The more people you meet, the more people you'll know," she says. "And the more people you know, the more people you'll meet."

A WORD TO THE WISE

For networking to be truly effective, it must become a way of life.

WHERE WILL I MEET THE PEOPLE I NEED TO MEET?

If you do all the right networking things, you should expect to meet people with whom you can network. If you join professional groups and clubs, attend conferences and seminars, and volunteer to help out at your library's annual book sale (more about all that in Chapter 12), it's a darn good bet you're going to be doing some networking.

Other times, you'll meet people without making an effort—it will just happen. The trick is to realize what's happening when it happens and to take advantage of the opportunity. Get out there and meet some people. You never know who they might be.

Colleges Are for Learning More than Math And Reading

If you're still in college, you have great possibilities for networking. The campus is a wonderful place to make connections that will last for the rest of your life. Look around you. Where do the rest of the students at your school come from?

If you're in a local or state college or university, other students probably are mostly from your own area or state. Such was the case with my college, Lock Haven University—most of the students were from Pennsylvania, but they were

---

> ## F.Y.I.
>
> Taking photos of guest speakers during luncheon and dinner presentations was one of my responsibilities when I worked in the public relations department of Kutztown State University. It was a job that some staff members tried to avoid, but I thought it provided wonderful opportunities to meet interesting people.
>
> I met people from different countries; people who were experts in obscure topics; and people who had worked with presidents, overcome addictions, lost their families to wars and civil strife, made discoveries, and flown in a small plane around the world. I always made a point to meet the speakers, introduce myself, and tell them how interesting their talks had been.
>
> The chicken and peas served at these events didn't make much of an impression, but the people I met there broadened and enriched my life—and my network.

from Philadelphia and Pittsburgh as well as suburban areas like where I grew up. There also were students who had grown up on farms in rural parts of the state. Some students had been raised very differently than I had been.

A really great thing about my university was, and still is, its commitment to foreign-exchange programs. I remember international students from Iran, Kenya, Cameroon, Ireland, England, Argentina, Poland, Germany, New Zealand, China, Chile, Cyprus, and Mexico—just to name a few places. What a wonderful opportunity! Foreign students, as you can well imagine, are eager to meet people and very willing to talk about their countries and families. I still keep in touch with several international students.

A Ready-Made Network

If you attend a major university that attracts students from all over the country and the world, you've got it made. Make the right connections, and you've got a big advantage. Maintain and nurture those connections, and you're way ahead on constructing a great network. Of course, if you sit in your room for four years, you can kiss any possible connections goodbye.

Join clubs. Perform in a play. Be a reporter for the college paper. Try out for a debate team. College is a great place to meet people and get connected, but it doesn't last forever. So get out of your room, and start meeting people!

Your Kids' Schools

If school or college is behind you, you've got a second chance to tap into the education connection via people at your children's schools. Kids are great for networking. They give you so many opportunities to meet someone without trying at all! When you get parents together who have kids of similar ages, they've always got something to talk about—their kids, of course.

You already read that your kids' friends' parents can be good networking contacts, but how do you go about meeting them? If you're sitting next to a woman you don't know, waiting for the school play to start, the most natural thing in the world is to ask what part her child has. She asks you the same thing, and the next thing you know, you've struck up a conversation. You learn each other's names and each other's children's names. She mentions that she hopes the play won't last more than an hour, because she has to get back to work. Naturally, you ask her where she works, and you find out she's the human resources manager at the largest industry in your area.

This conversation is really getting exciting for you, because you've been thinking about going back to work. After the play, you compliment her child's performance and tell her how much you've enjoyed meeting her before she rushes back to her office.

How do you make the most out of this opportunity? There are several ways.

- **Send a note with the cute photo of her daughter that you snapped during the play.** Tell her how much you enjoyed meeting her and you hope to see her at the next school function.
- **Look for her at the next event.** She'll no doubt thank you for the photo, thereby acknowledging that you've done her a favor. If you haven't been in touch since the school play, tell her how nice it is to see her again.
- **Keep in touch via your kids.** If you read something interesting about her child's teacher in the school district newsletter, for instance, clip it and send it to her with a little note. Say you thought she'd be interested and weren't sure whether she would have seen it.
- **Ask her to accompany you to another event.** After you've become better acquainted by seeing each other at a few school activities, you might ask her if she'd like to accompany you and your children to an evening book fair or another event.

Whatever you do, your goal is to turn a chance meeting into an enduring relationship. You want this woman as part of your network and probably as a friend, too. People are more willing to help someone they know than someone they don't know.

BE CAREFUL!

Never pretend to be a friend to someone because you want them to be a part of your network. Not everyone on your network will be—or should be—your friend.

If you act like a friend but your primary reason for making someone a part of your network is so he or she can help you get a job, your contact will end up feeling taken advantage of and used.

Kiddie Play Groups

If you have children who aren't in school yet, you still have opportunities to meet people. Play groups are disguised as opportunities for kids to get together and play, but they're really more for the parents, who get to enjoy some adult company while the kids play.

Typically, these groups are made up of mostly stay-at-home moms and their children. Many moms have taken time off from their careers to stay at home while the kids are young, and they are anxious to maintain contact with other professionals. Play groups are a great way to keep in touch with the professional world while making some new friends and contacts.

If you know about play groups in your area, find out who belongs and ask about joining one. If you don't know about any such groups, ask parents with kids around the same ages as yours if they would be interested in forming one. Chances are that the parents you talk to will know other parents who might also be interested. If you're new to the area, call the preschools and ask whether they know about any groups that meet informally.

Your Neighborhood

Many people don't even know their neighbors' names, much less how they spend their days. It is almost inconceivable to think that some of our best networking contacts might be living right across the street and we don't even know it, but it's entirely possible.

In Chapter 8, I suggested that you make a point to get to know your neighbors by having a picnic or a cocktail party. If you're not into hosting events, here are a few other suggestions:

- **Get a dog and walk it in your neighborhood every day.** You'll be amazed at what you see and who you might meet.
- **Plant some flowers in front of your house.** Flowers require tending, and the garden will make you accessible to any neighbors passing by.
- **Don't assume that your neighbors value their privacy over a friendly relationship.** In many of our neighborhoods, we've carried privacy to the extreme by constructing fences, planting hedges, and adding gates that keep the rest of the world out. Assume that your neighbor wants to get to know you. If he doesn't, he'll let you know.

Party Time

Social occasions are excellent opportunities for networking. People want to have a good time. They're friendly and relaxed, and open to talking to people they don't know.

Parties, weddings, bar mitzvahs, graduations, picnics, and other social events can open the door to meeting all sorts of interesting people who will make great additions to your network. There's just one thing. You can't sit in the corner, talking with the person you came with. Approaching people you don't know is an extremely difficult task for many people. Even experienced networkers sometimes don't want to do it.

Most of us look forward to parties as social events. We see friends—maybe some we haven't seen for a while—meet some new people, and before we know it, the evening's over and it's time to go home.

Some people look at parties a little bit differently. People who must attend parties because of their jobs or other obligations find that these social events can be a little wearing. Many of the people are there because they have to be there, not because they want to be. Most would rather be going home after a day in the office than making small talk with people they don't know.

Talking Up Strangers

Karen Kelly, the New York editorial director of Daybreak Books, attends many job-related parties when books are published and on other occasions. She has a rule that she tries to follow at each event: "I try to meet at least three new people at every party," she says. "That's the goal I set for myself, and then I can go home."

An experienced networker, Karen has some suggestions for people who are shy about approaching and starting conversations with strangers at parties or other social events:

- **Take a friend along.** It's often easier for two people to initiate a conversation with a stranger than it is for one person. A friend can fill in moments of silence, when you can't think of anything to say. Also, if the person you've approached rejects you by turning away to talk to someone else or leaving the area, you've still got your friend—"You're not just standing there by yourself with a drink in your hand."

- **Use humor when you meet someone for the first time.** Humor can be a great icebreaker, and it helps the person you're meeting remember you. "Once you've got someone to laugh, you've really gone halfway to being their friend," says Karen. You could make a funny comment about the ice sculpture or the party decorations as a means of starting a conversation. Be sure your comment is funny, not derogatory or offensive, and don't start off a conversation by telling a joke. People view that as being contrived and artificial.

- **Ask a lot of questions.** If you're nervous about meeting someone because you don't know what you'll say, ask questions. This method does several things for you: It makes you appear interested in the person you've just met, puts the burden of conversation on the other person, and opens the door to other topics. If someone says she has been with the present company for four years, then it's natural for you to ask where she was before that.

- **Approach someone you know who's talking to someone you don't know.** The person you know will probably introduce you to the person you don't know. So you've accomplished two things: You've touched base with someone you know—and perhaps haven't seen for a while—and you've met someone new. Approach the person to whom you've just been introduced again later, and continue a conversation or start a new one.

- **If you must go to a party by yourself, don't be one of the first people to arrive.** If you wait until the party is well under way, it will be more crowded and you'll feel less conspicuous. When you get there, take your time to scope out the situation. Hang up your coat and get a drink or something to eat.

Meanwhile, look around and see who's there, who's talking to who, and who is standing alone. It gives you time to make a plan.

- **Assume that people you have never met want to meet you and talk to you.** People are often reluctant to approach someone they don't know because they think they'll be bothering the person or intruding. Nonsense, Karen says. You're supposed to meet people at parties.

A WORD TO THE WISE

If you go to a party with a friend, your spouse, or someone else and want to do some networking while you're there, be sure that person realizes this ahead of time. "People always gravitate to people they know, and it's a waste of time if you're networking," says Karen Kelly, the New York editorial director of Daybreak Books. "Why spend all your time talking to someone you can talk to on the way home?"

At Work

If you have a job, you spend a lot of your time at your workplace. Many people spend more time at work than they do in their homes. For that reason, many of their networking happens on the job.

Networking in your own workplace is an often-overlooked opportunity. What can the people you already work with do for you? Well, that depends on who you work with. Keep your eyes open to networking opportunities at work. If someone asks you to make some copies, go ahead and do it—you never know who might be beside you, waiting to use the photocopier.

GIVE THANKS WHERE IT'S DUE

Some people are really lucky, because they were taught to network since they were kids. If your mom insisted you write thank-you notes every time you got a gift, thank her the next time you see her. If she encouraged you to have pen pals, read, and meet people, thank her profusely. If on top of all this she taught you good manners and the all-important skills of looking at someone when conversing, listening without interrupting, and caring about other people, thank her profusely *and* buy her some pretty flowers the next time you see her.

I'D LIKE YOU TO MEET

When Karen Kelly, the New York editorial director of Daybreak Books, was just starting out in the publishing industry, she was hired as an assistant editor. People who had been with the company for a while noticed that she was an enthusiastic and willing employee who was willing to work hard. That being the case, Karen was assigned a lot of tasks that weren't part of her job description. "All of a sudden, I was making up budgets," she says. "It was really funny, because I didn't know the first thing about them."

Still, Karen had been assigned budgets, and she was determined to do the job right. She asked around for help and eventually linked up with the company's chief financial officer (CFO). He said he was too busy to help her during the workday, but it was his habit to get to his office early in the morning. If she would be willing to come in early, he could help her before starting work.

Karen started showing up at 7 a.m., and the CFO let her use his computer. She would work for two hours, aided by the expertise of the CFO, who drank coffee and read the newspaper during that time. Karen completed the budgets and got noticed as a smart worker who was willing to go the extra mile. She also became good friends with the CFO. Years later, they remain friends.

Mothers can start teaching children good networking skills when they are very young. Of course, a mom would never sit her kid down and say, "Today I'm going to teach you the basics of networking"; instead, she teaches manners and social skills, which are very important tools in networking.

Use those skills, and keep alert to opportunities. If you're not looking for them, you're going to miss them.

Networking Notes

- Possibilities to network arise constantly, but you have to be aware of them and take advantage of them when they do.
- Some networking opportunities are planned, but many occur when you least expect them.
- Schools and colleges are great places to make contacts.
- Parents' networking opportunities abound at young children's play groups.
- There probably are chances for networking right outside your door, in your own neighborhood.
- To meet people at a party, bring a friend to help you, say something funny, ask a lot of questions, get someone else at the party to introduce you, and assume that people want to meet you.
- If you already have a job, some of your best chances for networking might be right under your nose. Or in the copy room.

CHAPTER | 12

USING ORGANIZATIONS AND CLUBS TO EXPAND YOUR NETWORK

Thes groups are part of the networking equation too? You bet. Professional groups, social clubs, civic organizations, and alumni organizations are extremely important to networks and should not be overlooked.

You probably know people who belong to clubs. They might have a lunch group on Tuesdays, Rotary meetings on Wednesday nights, and after-work get-togethers with the office on Fridays. Unless these people are sitting on their hands with their lips sealed, it's a good bet that there's a fair amount of networking taking place during these outings. Clubs and organizations are great places to network for several reasons:

- The other people share your interests.
- Members are usually sociable types who are eager to meet and talk with others.
- The members form relationships and develop loyalty toward the organization and each other.

- As loyalty develops, members want other members of their clubs and organizations to succeed and will help them to do so.

If you don't belong to any clubs or organizations, think about what kinds of groups you might like to join. If nothing else, attending meetings gets you out of the house and around people. Remember: You can't network with your television set.

PROFESSIONAL GROUPS

In addition to being good places to meet people, professional clubs and organizations often provide lists of job opportunities, and some even offer job placement assistance. How do you find out what professional clubs are available, and how do you go about joining one?

You should join a group intended for members of either the profession you're working in or the one you want to be working in. There are several ways to find these groups, but getting referrals from members probably is best. If you're interested in teaching, for instance, ask some teachers for the names of the professional groups they belong to. If you are a computer programmer, your best source is someone working in the computer industry.

Don't hesitate to ask people for this kind of information. Most are happy to help and will be glad to not only give you the names of the organizations and their officers but also tell you when and where the group meets.

If you don't know anyone who might belong to a professional group in your area, check your area's telephone directory. Many organizations are listed. Your local chamber of commerce also may have information about professional organizations. Search the Internet—many organizations have Web sites, and even if they're not in your area, the listings will give you some idea what kinds of groups are available.

If you can't find a group using those resources, your local library should be able to help. Look for the following books:

- *The Encyclopedia of Associations,* a multi-volume resource from Gale Research, Inc. (Detroit, MI), lists the names of more than 25,000 associations and non-profit groups. Ask the reference librarian to show you how to use the encyclopedia.

- *Regional, State, and Local Organizations,* also published by Gale Research, lists more than 50,000 organizations at the state, regional, and local levels.
- *Career Guide to Professional Associations: A Directory of Organizations by Occupational Field,* published by Carroll Press (Evanston, RI), lists more than 2,500 organizations for a variety of job areas.
- *National Trade and Professional Associations of the United States,* from Columbia Books (New York), includes the names of more than 7,000 associations, along with their publications and primary contacts.

When you locate information about a group that suits your needs and interests, call its main office. Ask for the name of the president of your local chapter, who can tell you where and when the group meets and most likely will invite you to the next meeting.

What To Do When You Get There

Take advantage of the opportunities the group will offer. The number of professional groups has been increasing over the past decade by about 10 percent a year, and for good reason.

Members of professional groups share ideas and resources and can refer each other to people of similar interests who are members of other groups. Many groups offer training, seminars, and conferences. Professional organizations provide access to people you might not easily meet otherwise.

Gale Ross, an independent contractor who writes computer hardware and software programs, attends meetings of the Society of Technical Communicators near her home in Andover, Massachusetts, to meet new people within her field and keep up with opportunities, trends, and news. She claims that being active in such organizations is important, regardless of whether you're just starting a career or already well established. She offers some suggestions for people joining professional organizations:

- **If you're nervous about attending meetings and activities by yourself, ask a friend to go with you.** Just remember that you're there to meet people and find out what's going on, not chat with your friend.
- **Take plenty of business cards, and don't be shy about handing them out.** A lot of introductions are made during these meetings. Don't assume that people will remember your name if you don't give them your card.

- **Have a résumé stashed away in your car, purse, or briefcase, just in case.** Recruiters and hiring managers often attend professional meetings and just might be interested in learning more about you.

After you've been in a professional group for a while and you understand the organization and structure, volunteer to serve on some committees or run for office. Your increased participation gives you greater visibility within the organization and can link you to other organizations.

A WORD TO THE WISE

Don't be shy when attending meetings of professional groups. You want to come off looking and sounding confident and self-assured. Dress and behave professionally. Tell people about yourself, and introduce yourself in a way that makes people interested in you. For instance, instead of saying, "I work for a newspaper," say "I write that financial column that's on the business page of *The Times* every Thursday." The additional information will make you more interesting and memorable to the person you're meeting.

PROFESSIONAL CONFERENCES, SEMINARS, AND TRADE SHOWS

These are some of the best places to meet new people who may benefit you in your career. You should always be on the lookout for people with whom you'd like to network at these gatherings; don't overlook the speakers and instructors!

If you go to a lot of conferences or trade shows, you'll start to see the same people over and over again. Always take the opportunity to follow up with someone you met at a previous show. Many good networkers follow up with people they meet at conferences or shows when they get back to their offices. They'll send a note saying something like this:

It was really nice meeting you last week at the conference in New Orleans. I thoroughly enjoyed our talk about the future of the industry, and I hope we'll have a chance to talk about it more sometime. Will you by any chance be attending the seminar next month in Phoenix? If so, maybe we can catch up there.

One of the major advantages of attending these events is that you meet many people within your field. If you should suddenly find yourself out of work or looking for a new job, you will have made contacts within your industry.

Be sure to file all the business cards you get at conferences and trade shows, and always have plenty of your cards with you. Note any particular details about the people you meet on the backs of their cards.

CONTINUING EDUCATION

Continuing education courses, career development programs, and enrichment programs can be great sources of networking connections.

Amy Weston is a technical director for Pacific Bell in Pleasanton, California. As manager of a group of programmers and business analysts for software development, she has hired numerous people—many of whom she met at or through school. Amy recently met a woman while attending a week-long class at University of California–Los Angeles. The woman's husband was looking for a position as a systems architect in Northern California, and Amy was looking to hire someone. "We checked out his résumé, flew him up, and hired him," she says. "He's terrific and working out great."

Amy says that the networking value of such courses lies in the fact that most of the people in them are working in the same field and willing to share ideas and referrals. "Taking classes is a great way to network because you can focus in on subject matter particular to your area and meet many interesting people who can give you great ideas," she explains.

NETWORKING GROUPS

A growing number of groups are designed specifically for the purpose of networking. Members, most of whom are small business owners or professionals—mortgage bankers, accountants, insurance brokers, graphic designers, chiropractors, and stockbrokers—use these groups to give and receive referrals.

A well-known group of this type is LeTip, a nationwide referral organization with more than 10,000 members in 500 chapters across the country. LeTip was started in San Diego in 1978 by an insurance broker who realized that many business people had mutual needs for referral business. Many members of these groups swear by them; some say as much as half their business is generated by group referrals.

SOCIAL CLUBS

These groups are very different from professional organizations, but don't think that social clubs don't involve networking—they offer excellent opportunities. Lunch clubs, golf clubs, card clubs, and dinner clubs are the places at which information is shared, deals are made, and lasting friendships are forged.

If networking sometimes seems like a cold and calculating method of meeting people to you, then the concept of social clubs should put you at ease. Members of the same club often develop great loyalty toward their club and each other. The networking that occurs within the club is natural and genuine.

Say, for example, that you've played tennis in the same foursome for nine years: Ted, Danny, Mike, and you, every Wednesday night for nine years. You've played a lot of doubles together, drank a lot of beers afterwards, and done some pretty intense bonding. When Danny had his knee operated on, the other three of you gave up your court time to visit him; you all saw Mike through his divorce; and they were there for you when you were laid off in a company downsizing. You've celebrated births, mourned at funerals, sent get-well cards, and gathered together with your significant others for dinners and cookouts.

That doubles group is pretty tight. So, when you get a hot tip about a job opening in your company, you don't keep it to yourself. You get on the phone to Danny, who's been unhappy with his job situation and looking for something else. Who knows—your tennis partner might become your new coworker.

Social clubs foster good will among members because the members share a common bond. You're all in something together; it creates security and comfort. It's only natural to want to help somebody you're comfortable with and enjoy spending time with.

SPECIAL INTEREST

As a feature writer for a newspaper, I wrote many stories about groups in which members pursued common interests. One story I remember about a group of retired men and women whose common interest was a stretch of the Appalachian Trail. These men and women were self-appointed guardians of "their" section of the trail. They had no obligation to see to its upkeep; it was just something they did. Most of them had lived near the trail for their entire lives, and they were passionate about keeping it well maintained and litter free.

As a result of their involvement in the Trailkeepers (their name for their group), these men and women met hikers from all over the country and from other countries, as well. Often, they'd get to talking with some hikers and invite them home for a home-cooked meal and a shower (two great luxuries to somebody who's been on the trail for a while).

These retirees weren't networking for job leads, nor were they looking for favors in return for their kindness. The interesting people they met simply added to the richness of their lives.

Another special interest group I remember was an organization of rose enthusiasts. The men and women in this group, a local chapter of the American Rose Society, certainly loved roses. They attended and sponsored rose shows, toured various areas to view roses, and assisted less talented rose growers in their gardens. They networked constantly about their roses. The group was interesting because it included a cross-section of young and old, male and female rose lovers from various social backgrounds.

Special interest groups like these are as varied as the people who form them. They all provide opportunities for networking and meeting people. So, be alert and receptive to groups and clubs of all kinds as possibilities for improving your network.

CIVIC, COMMUNITY, AND CHARITABLE ORGANIZATIONS

Participation in civic, community, and charitable organizations also offers excellent networking opportunities.

The next time your local United Way kicks off its annual fundraising drive, read about it in your newspaper. Who's the campaign chairperson? You can bet it's not somebody you've never heard of, but chances are good that it's a high-profile, influential member of the community.

The United Way campaign is a massive undertaking that requires volunteer help at every level and the participation of a lot of business and community leaders. It's a perfect opportunity for you to get involved, meet people, and develop some networking contacts. At the same time, your community will benefit.

In every community, there are dozens of opportunities to make valuable contacts while doing good for someone else. Several organizations probably have local chapters near you:

- Lions Club
- Rotary Club
- Kiwanis Club

- roadway clean-up crew
- neighborhood crime watch
- community anniversary committee
- American Red Cross
- March of Dimes
- Easter Seals

Organizations like these are always looking for volunteers and new members. Get involved, and get active. As you meet people, watch for opportunities to make contacts with members of other organizations or people with whom your organization has contact.

F.Y.I.

Professional golfer Betsy King grew up in the area where I live, and three years ago, the Ladies Professional Golf Association established a tournament here in King's name. The tournament draws some big-name women golfers and is a source of community excitement and pride.

In addition to hundreds of volunteers, major corporations and small businesses alike get involved with the event. The volunteer corps is a great mix of people who represent community groups, businesses, and corporations. They have a great opportunity to meet and network with a lot of people. They also get to watch some great golf and maybe even rub elbows with the professionals.

Volunteer work, although rewarding unto itself, has often led to jobs as a result of getting to know the right people. If you volunteer to help within an organization or event, take your work seriously, and do the best you can. If you volunteer to do a job but don't show up for the meetings or to help with an event, you will be labeled as an undependable person.

All you need to do to find out about volunteer opportunities in your area is to pick up your phone book. Many communities have volunteer placement centers, and some newspapers list groups that need volunteers. Once you get involved, you'll have the double satisfaction of helping out in your community and expanding your network.

I'D LIKE YOU TO MEET

Mary Diaz, the executive director of the Women's Commission for Refugee Women and Children in New York City, comes from a family that stressed volunteerism and service. She left a job in Philadelphia as a news writer and associate producer for a major television station to work at the Catholic Charities Refugee Services in Boston, Massachusetts. She later was named director of the Women's Commission, an advocacy and policy-making organization that works with the United Nations and the State Department to achieve decent conditions for women and children refugees. She has traveled to war-torn countries to get a firsthand look at conditions and finds the work immensely rewarding.

This job also comes with a fringe benefit of great networking opportunities. In addition to meeting people at the various agencies and organizations with which she works, Mary meets many celebrities who lend their names and energies to the cause. Among those associated with her organization are Liv Ullman (honorary chairwoman); Meredith Brokaw, wife of newsman Tom Brokaw; Meryl Streep; Vanessa Redgrave; Sam Watterson; and Suzy Buffet, wife of Warren Buffet.

Mary says she used to be extremely nervous around these high-profile people but now has relaxed and enjoys their company. She finds it extremely interesting to interact and network with such people for a common cause.

ALUMNI ORGANIZATIONS

Alumni organizations are among the very best sources of networking opportunities. Given the opportunity, make sure to take advantage. Members of alumni groups want to see fellow graduates succeed, and many will go to great lengths to ensure that they do.

If your college sends out notices about alumni meetings in various areas, take notice and try to attend one that's being held near you. You'll not only make some good contacts, you'll probably have a great time meeting people who graduated from the same school.

FRATERNITIES AND SORORITIES

If you are a member of a fraternity or sorority, you have a built-in network for life. Great bonding goes on within these organizations, and members do well to keep in touch with one another after they leave college because they can help each other immensely. Because many fraternities and sororities are national or even international organizations, networking opportunities reach far beyond the brothers or sisters from your own school.

Imagine an employer looking at the résumés from the top two candidates for a position. The candidates are evenly matched, and he's just about ready to flip a coin. "But wait!" he says. "This guy was a member of Tau Kappa Epsilon. Why, that's *my* fraternity!"

Who do you think got the job?

Networking Notes

- Professional groups, social clubs, alumni organizations, and community organizations offer excellent networking possibilities.
- Obtain names of professional groups from members of the profession or locate group names in your phone book, on the Internet, or from directories at your local library.
- Once you've joined a professional group, try to get appointed to a committee or become an officer. Increased participation gives you more visibility and connections.
- Professional conferences, seminars, and trade shows provide extensive opportunities for networking. Remember to bring business cards.
- Continuing education classes and career training programs also are good places to network with people whose interests are similar to yours.
- Social clubs, although less structured than professional organizations, are good places for natural networking.
- Members of special interest groups—such as those for plant enthusiasts or stamp collectors—often are of varying ages, backgrounds, and social status.
- Civic, community, and charitable organizations often include high-profile members of the community; they offer opportunities to meet people and always are looking for volunteers.
- Alumni organizations and fraternities and sororities offer ready-made networking opportunities.

CHAPTER | 13

FOLLOWING UP AFTER YOU'RE CONNECTED

You've been working hard to make connections for your network, and it's starting to pay off. The length of your networking list is increasing every day, and you've started getting a few calls back from people you've contacted. Nice job!

There's just one problem. Once you've made contacts and gotten connected, how do you stay connected? I mean, you're not the only bright, eager, and willing wannabe networker out there. Assuming that your résumé (and 20 other unsolicited résumés) makes it from the top of someone's desk to the résumé file, what can you do to make sure the person you contacted remembers you?

Your work doesn't end when you make a contact. Making contact merely establishes a base. It's a very important step, but without regular follow-up, that connection won't last. You have to set yourself apart from the competition.

Barbara Turkington is an independent marketing consultant in Boston, Massachusetts. She makes a point of staying in contact with all her clients and other business associates because she finds there is a lot of truth in the old adage, "out of sight, out of mind."

An experienced networker and established businesswoman, Barbara has no illusions that people, even her clients, will remember her without prompting. "I send out notes to remind people of my existence," she says. "It amazes me how quickly people forget about me and my services." Neither should you.

AFTER THE INITIAL CONTACT—NOW WHAT?

You've sent out dozens of résumés and made dozens of follow-up phone calls. You did your homework in preparing for job interviews and sent out thank-you notes when they were over. You've worked hard, but if the people you met don't remember you, then all that hard work will have been for nothing!

Don't worry. We're not going to let that happen. You just need to learn how to stay in touch once you've gotten connected. Consider the following scenario.

What Went Wrong?

John did everything right when he set up his informational interview with Ms. Keller, the accounting supervisor of the XYZ Company. First, he sent a letter of introduction, giving her a little information about his background and requesting a meeting for the purpose of an informational interview. He said he'd call her the following week.

John called the following week, and again, he did everything right. He introduced himself to Ms. Keller and said he hoped she had received his letter. He reminded her that he had asked for 15 minutes of her time for an informational interview, and he assured her that he was not requesting a job interview. Ms. Keller said she would be happy to meet with him, and he prepared diligently for the interview. He learned all he could about the XYZ Company—he even found an item in a past edition of his local paper that announced Ms. Keller's promotion to supervisor.

John had prepared a brief overview of his goals, and Ms. Keller seemed genuinely interested in what he had to say. He asked great questions about her job, the company, and the accounting field in general. The 15-minute meeting stretched to nearly half an hour, and Ms. Keller could not have been any nicer.

John sent Ms. Keller a sincere thank-you note the day after the meeting, and he really had a good feeling about things. In the back of his mind, John was expecting to hear back from her.

The problem is, the meeting was two weeks ago, and John hasn't heard a word. Can it be that his informational interview hadn't gone as well as he thought?

Don't Relax Yet!

Arranging and conducting the informational interview is a big step, but it is just the beginning of the networking effort. John has to realize that Ms. Keller has no obligation to get back to him; it's his job to keep in touch with her.

What John should have done as he wrapped up his informational interview was pave the way for a follow-up. He could have said something like, "Ms. Keller, I've really enjoyed talking with you today. May I keep in touch with you? I'd like to give you a call in a couple of weeks and keep you up-to-date with my job search." If John's meeting with Ms. Keller went as well as he thought, chances are that she'll be happy to hear from him again. If she says okay, then John can feel comfortable calling her in a couple of weeks, just to touch base.

If John didn't set the stage for a follow-up, he can call anyway. When calling, he should remind Ms. Keller of their meeting, thank her again for taking the time, and ask if it would be okay for him to keep her informed of his job hunt.

If John didn't give Ms. Keller his résumé before, this would be a good time to do so. He may or may not have given her a copy during the informational interview. If she was interested and asked for a copy, he certainly should have had one available, but he may not have wanted to offer one because he wasn't asking for a job, and a résumé could indicate different intentions.

Now that the informational interview is over, John needs to make sure that Ms. Keller will remember him. He should send his résumé along with a note reminding her of their meeting. In it, he could say that he thought she might be interested in seeing a copy of the résumé and that he would welcome any comments or suggestions about it. This gives Ms. Keller a chance to get a better idea of John's background, and something on the résumé might trigger an idea of another person John could contact or even a job opportunity.

BE CAREFUL!

While John can feel free to call, he has to be careful he doesn't make a pest of himself by overdoing it. He might follow up with a phone call in a couple of weeks, then wait for a month before calling again. He wants to get established in Ms. Keller's mind, not annoy her with too-frequent phone calls.

A WORD TO THE WISE

Always include a business card with correspondence. If your business card ends up in your contact person's card file, you've become part of that person's network. He or she will see your name in the file, and you'll be remembered. If your business card ends up in the trash can, though, all you've lost is a card.

Ask for Advice

Let's get a bit more creative and think of some other ways that John might keep in touch with Ms. Keller. If something significant develops in John's job search, he might call her to ask her opinion. For example, if he is offered a job that he doesn't really want and he's not sure whether it would be a good career move for him to take it, he could call to ask her advice. She probably would be flattered.

Barbara Turkington says she often sought advice from contacts. "I would compile a list of contacts and call them to ask for their help. I didn't put them on the defensive by asking for a job, I simply asked them for guidance," she says. "Most people, even busy executives, are willing to help someone who asks for it."

Write a Note

Most people enjoy getting a personal note from someone they've met. John might tell Ms. Keller that he has had two more informational interviews since theirs and that he thought they went well. If he has contacted someone Ms. Keller had told him about, he could mention that as well:

> *I dropped a note to Mr. Gary a couple of weeks ago and followed up with a phone call on June 21. I told him, as you said I could, that you had given me his name. He was quite interested to hear how I had met you, and he had some very nice things to say about you.*

In his note to Ms. Keller, John achieves several things:
1. Keeping in touch.
2. Informing her that he's used her name when contacting someone else.
3. Establishing a history with her. By telling Ms. Keller that he and Mr. Gary had talked about her, he's implying that he's part of their network; he's making their network part of his network.

John not only uses an effective method of keeping in touch but also is courteous in letting Ms. Keller know that he used her name. By doing so, he prepares Ms. Keller for her next meeting with Mr. Gary.

Be Enthusiastic and Positive

As part of his efforts to network, John is having coffee one morning with Jenny, who works for a company located near Ms. Keller's office. He sees Ms. Keller come into the coffee shop and walk straight to the take-out counter.

It would be remiss for John to not take advantage of the opportunity for a face-to-face meeting with Ms. Keller. He should very politely excuse himself ("I'm so sorry, would you excuse me for just a moment, please? Someone just came in who I really need to have a word with."), then approach Ms. Keller. John should flash his best smile, offer his hand, and be enthusiastic about seeing her again.

F.Y.I.

Remember that there's a fine line between enthusiastic and over-bearing; be friendly, but in a courteous and professional way.

Look for Interesting Articles and Other Information

If John sees an article in a business journal about a topic he and Ms. Keller discussed during their informational interview, it would be perfectly acceptable (not to mention smart) for him to send it to her with a short note:

> I thought you might be interested in reading this article. As you recall, we discussed this topic during our meeting on June 12. The author's opinion is quite different than yours, isn't it?

Ms. Keller will not only appreciate getting a copy of the article, she'll most likely be flattered that John remembered her opinion on this topic.

Sending bits and pieces of interesting information is a great way to stay in touch with a contact. Say for instance, that Ms. Keller had mentioned to John that she was leaving shortly after their meeting for a weekend of skiing, her favorite hobby. John would be within bounds if he later sent her a clipping about a fancy new ski resort opening near their city, along with a note. He would be thoroughly out of bounds, however, if he suggested that he and Ms. Keller check out the new resort together!

> *I hope you enjoyed your skiing weekend. I didn't know whether you*
> *had heard about this planned resort. Thought you might be interested.*

Again, Ms. Keller probably will be flattered that John thought about her in connection with skiing, and she's likely to remember him as being a thoughtful, considerate person.

Following Up with Phone Contacts

If you've made a contact over the telephone but haven't met your contact in person, follow-up is more important than ever. A busy person might talk on the phone to how many people in one day—6? 12? 20? One phone call isn't enough to keep your contact alive.

In Chapter 10, I presented a hypothetical phone conversation with Mr. Jones. You asked him for the names of newspaper editors with whom you might get in touch, and he said he'd get back to you with the names. Hopefully, that's just what he did. If you didn't hear from him within a week or so, you should have called back to remind him, very nicely, that you were waiting for those names. You should have said that you knew he was very busy and really appreciated the time he'd taken to help you. Then, you should have asked if he needed more time and if you could call him for the names at the end of the week.

Whenever you get the names from Mr. Jones, be sure to follow up with a thank-you note and send him a copy of your résumé (if he doesn't have one already). This not only gives him more information about you but also allows him to talk about you in an informed manner to the people he referred you to.

If you make contact with someone on the list of names Mr. Jones provided, be sure to let him know in a short note like this one:

> *I just thought you'd be interested in knowing that I met Mr. Smith in*
> *his office yesterday morning. Although he doesn't have any openings at*
> *this time, he promised to keep my résumé handy and let me know if*
> *something comes up. Thanks again for the reference.*

If you wait another week and still haven't heard from Mr. Jones, call him again, or send him a note reminding him. You can be persistent without alienating someone if you are polite and respectful. However, if it gets to the point where you've called Mr. Jones 16 times and he *still* has no names for you, maybe you'd better figure he's really not interested.

A WORD TO THE WISE

When you're networking, keep the ball in your court as often as possible. If a contact says he'll call you back with information, offer to call him instead. If he insists that he'll call you, say something like, "That would be great, I really appreciate it. If for some reason I miss your call, would it be okay if I get back to you at the end of the week?"

This keeps you in control of the situation instead of at the mercy of the other person.

Following Up with A Face-to-Face Contact

If you've met someone in person with whom you hope to network, you can follow up in much the same way John did with Ms. Keller. A thank-you note for the meeting is always in order, as is supplying a résumé and business card. Keep your contact informed of your progress, send interesting clippings or articles, and be friendly and positive when you see your contact again, and you'll be almost assured of keeping that connection active.

Thanks!

If advice or information that a contact gives you leads directly to a job, you should follow up. If you've been keeping your contact informed about the status of your job hunt, then he or she will know that you were close to being hired. Perhaps you said that you had an interview scheduled or that you had already had an interview.

If you are offered a job and want to get your contact's opinion before you accept, go ahead. After all, it was his or her lead that got you this far. He or she might be able to offer some insights or recommend some questions for you to ask. Don't ask your contact for advice about whether to accept the job, however, if you have no intention of listening to that advice. So, if you've already decided not to accept the position, don't call and ask your contact what he or she thinks you should do.

Instead, do your contact the courtesy of calling him or her to say you were offered the job but declined for certain reasons, and explain exactly what those reasons are. If your contact feels very strongly that this job is perfect for you, he or she might try to change your mind. You might be surprised and end up deciding to take the job after all. If not, thank your contact politely for his or her input and say that you've made up your mind that this is not the job for you.

If you've accepted the job, call your contact to tell him or her the news and express your thanks again for the referral. He or she will appreciate that you took the time to call and tell the news first-hand.

Keeping in Touch Once You Have the Job

If you're in a position to do so, and you feel it's appropriate, you might ask your contact to lunch as a thank you. Send a note after you've been on the job for a couple of weeks. Include one of your business cards, and say how well you're doing. Follow up in a couple of months, saying how well things are going and how much you appreciate his or her help in finding this great job.

Things could get a little tricky if for some reason the job doesn't work out but you want to keep your contact as part of your network. If such a situation should arise, call your contact directly and explain why you left (or lost) the job. Be forthright and honest, but don't give more information than you need to. For instance, if you didn't get along with your boss (your contact's friend), just say that the job wasn't what you had expected. It won't do you any good to get on the phone and complain that your contact's friend of 25 years was mean to you and wouldn't give you the days off that he had promised.

INGREDIENTS FOR A SUCCESSFUL FOLLOW-UP

Keeping in touch with contacts you've made isn't difficult, but it does require organization, persistence, a little creativity, and common sense.

Organization

Organization is important because without it, you'll find it difficult to remember what you've done, what you haven't, and for whom. It is important to keep detailed records of when you talk or meet with someone and to keep track of what follow-up is expected after your conversation or meeting.

- Ms. Keller will appreciate the article about the new ski resort, but she will not be pleased to receive two or three copies of the same thing because you forgot whether you had already mailed it.
- If you meant to write Mr. Jones a note informing him of your meeting with Mr. Smith but never get around to it, your good intentions were wasted.

- You'll lose credibility if you say you'll return a phone call on a certain day but forget to put it on your calendar.
- If you write a great thank-you note but don't mail it, you might as well not bother writing it at all.

Persistence

Persistence is required when following up with your contacts because you might not always get the cooperation you hope for. If someone doesn't return your calls after four messages, write a note and then try calling again.

If someone agrees to meet you for an informational interview but cancels at the last minute because "something came up," you'll need to call back to reschedule the meeting. You can't be timid or give up easily when networking.

Creativity

Anyone can write a note or pick up the phone. How do you make your follow-up something that your contact will remember? Be creative, that's how.

Your notes and phone conversations should be as interesting as possible. Instead of responding "not much" when Mr. Jones asks you what you've been doing, say something like this:

> Mr. Jones, I've been turning this town upside down, looking for leads in my job search. So far, none have been as good as those that you've given me.

Instead of answering "okay" or "just fine" when Mr. Jones asks how you are, say something like this:

> Mr. Jones, I'm just fine, thank you. I am having a great time tracking down these leads. I've met some of the most interesting people!

Upbeat, positive answers make you appear as an upbeat, positive person—the kind of person that others like to be around. Apply the same principle to the notes and cards you write. A thank-you card is nice, but an exciting thank-you message is memorable. Which do you think would be remembered?

Dear Ms. Keller,

Thank you very much for meeting with me on Thursday. I enjoyed meeting you and I appreciate that you took your time to answer my questions....

Or

Dear Ms. Keller,

I certainly enjoyed our meeting on Thursday. Thank you very much for giving me some of your time. I especially enjoyed hearing your views on upcoming trends in the accounting field. You obviously have done your homework....

Think about other creative and innovative ways to stay in touch with your contacts. Just a word, though: Don't go overboard or do something that's really over the edge. Sending a framed photograph of yourself to someone would attract attention, all right, but not the sort of attention that's going to help you get a job.

Common Sense and Courtesy

Good old common sense and courtesy will help you be a successful networker as much as anything else.

If a potential contact doesn't return your phone calls—repeatedly—try to find out why. Perhaps there has been a miscommunication. Maybe that person doesn't have the correct phone number. If you want to know what's going on, ask the person who answers your call why your call isn't getting through.

Use your judgment to determine how you should relate to the people with whom you're trying to stay connected. Some people prefer a casual style, and you can interact with them in a more friendly, relaxed manner than with others. Make sure you know who you're dealing with before you start making jokes or assume that you're on a first-name basis. If everyone calls your new contact "Mr. Smith," it won't do for you to start calling him "Harold."

If someone does something nice for you, thank them. If somebody does something really nice for you, thank them profusely. One good turn deserves another! Let common sense and courtesy guide you.

Networking Notes

- Never assume that people will remember you once you've contacted them—you have to make an effort to stay connected.
- It's up to you to stay in touch.
- Be creative when looking for ways to stay in touch with someone. Ask for advice or send an interesting article, for example.
- Be positive and upbeat when you interact with a contact.
- Always let a contact know if a reference or a tip he or she gave you results in a job or an offer.
- Common sense and courtesy are the guidelines to use when making and maintaining contact with people you want in your network.

CHAPTER | 14

YOUR NETWORK SHOULD NEVER STOP EXPANDING

After you've been at this for a while, you'll stop and realize that you have a good, solid network in place. It includes people you work with, people you used to work with, and a whole bunch of people from groups you belong to (professional organizations, social clubs, your neighborhood, your place of worship, and so on). You have networking connections that you can call on in a variety of situations—when you need to find a job or a good plumber.

Whew! It's hard work putting together a network, but you've done it. The card file is up-to-date and organized, the latest batch of birthday cards has been mailed, and your membership card for that professional organization just arrived in the mail. Time to relax and enjoy the benefits, right?

Wrong. Guess what? Networking is one of those jobs that never ends. It's like lawn care: You cut your grass, trim the hedges, plant some flowers, and mulch the garden, then you sit down with a tall glass of lemonade to enjoy the view. Before you even finish the lemonade, the grass is high again, the hedges have sprouted anew, the flowers need to be watered, and weeds are poking up through the mulch. Time to get back to work.

HOW TO ENLARGE YOUR NETWORK

If you meet new people all the time, then your network should never stop growing. If you don't meet new people regularly, maybe you have to start doing something differently.

Say you have a job that requires you to call people every day—each call is a perfect opportunity for networking. Maybe you work in an office where people are in and out all day—same thing. Health care, teaching, sales, and many other jobs give you the opportunity to meet many people.

The trick is to not only meet people but also figure out ways to establish relationships. Of course, you can't connect with every single person you meet, or you'd have a card file the size of a Volkswagen! Just be open to what people have to offer and what you can offer them. Be on the lookout whenever you meet someone, and don't forget to target people you'd like to meet.

Meeting New People

If you don't meet new people regularly, ask yourself, "Why not?" Do you not have the opportunity to make new contacts, or do you not take advantage of the opportunities you do have? A composer, for example, who sits at the piano composing concertos all day, every day, will meet fewer people than a receptionist in a busy doctor's office.

Meetings are not limited to work. You might work all day and not meet many new people. It's pretty much the same group, all the time. What you need to do in that case is think creatively. How can you break out of your routine? Here are some suggestions:

- **Take advantage of your lunch hour.** Some communities cater to the lunch crowd by offering free concerts or other events in public places during the noon hour. Find out what's available, and take advantage. Even getting out for a walk or doing some errands puts you in a position to meet people; sitting in your office doing the brown bag thing does not.

- **Take a walk.** Use your break or lunch hour to get out. Besides making you more alert and healthy, a brisk walk might present opportunities to meet people. You never know who else might be out getting some exercise.
- **Investigate another part of your building.** What other offices are there in your building? If you're in a professional office building, you have lots of people within shouting distance who might be valuable additions to your network. Get out in the hallway and talk to people. Where's the drinking fountain? The rest rooms? If your entire building is one company, find an excuse to visit another department now and then.
- **Visit the fitness center.** More and more companies are setting up in-house fitness centers for employees, which offer a perfect opportunity to meet people and establish some new networking partners. If you like to do aerobics, suggest starting an aerobics group and volunteer to alternate providing the tape and leading the class. It's more fun to exercise with other people, and you'll end up making some friends.
- **Buy some candy.** I've never worked in an office where employees didn't sell stuff for their kids—Girl Scout cookies, candy bars, honey-roasted peanuts. The next time you see something for sale, buy it, and make sure you hand-deliver the payment to the person selling it. You might want to consider giving the candy to someone else, though—good will takes its toll on your hips!
- **Make some plans for after work.** What do the people in your office do after work—ever ask? Invite a coworker to go for a drink or for a walk. Social connections often turn out to be valuable members of our networks.

Advice for Those at Home

Stay-at-home moms, househusbands, retired people, and home-based workers who spend much of their time at home often complain of feeling isolated and out of touch. It's true that being at home all day can be restricting, especially if you have an infant to care for or are physically unable to get around.

Unless you are physically restricted or you live in a rural area and don't have a car, there are ways you can get out and meet people. If you live in the middle of nowhere without a car, why not call a couple of moms and invite them over for coffee? Creative people, regardless of the situation, find ways to keep up with existing contacts and make new ones. Here are some suggestions:

- **Take walks.** Walking through your neighborhood is a great way to meet people. You have to be friendly and willing to make the first move when you see people along the way. One of my favorite methods of meeting people who are working in their yards is to compliment their efforts. "Your garden looks so pretty," I'll call to someone who is weeding a garden. "What kind of flowers are they?" In addition to paying someone a compliment and acknowledging their work, it opens up the door to a conversation. You'll meet a neighbor and learn something about gardening, too.

- **Start a social group.** If you're feeling isolated because of your situation, it's a good bet that others in the same situation feel similarly. Take a chance. Be the one that gets on the phone and organizes something. How about a book discussion group, a dining club, or a bowling league? They're great for creating camaraderie. What about a walking group? Three or four stay-at-home parents get together and take turns being responsible for child care while the others walk. There are lots of ways to meet people in similar situations, but assume you'll have to be the one to initiate it.

- **Organize a co-op.** Find out the names of other people in your area or your apartment building who are at home with kids during the day. Talk to people. If you know one person, he or she probably knows somebody else. If there's a preschool in your area, you might be able to get some names there. Once you have a list, get on the phone and see if there's interest in starting a babysitting co-op. You get to know people quickly when you're working together to organize something. You'll be adding new people to your network and doing something that's beneficial for everyone—including you.

- **Start a home-based business.** Do you love to cook? Do your friends rave about your dinner parties? Spread the word that you'll make that fabulous chicken dish for their parties. Send around a flyer in your neighborhood offering to do yard work for a reasonable fee—many people are glad for the help. Check out the Internet; there are lots of sites for people wanting to start home-based businesses. Visit your local library for books or guides, or call your local chamber of commerce. Some chambers offer free help to people interested in starting businesses.

Whatever you do, do something that will get you in contact with other people. Being sociable and friendly is a big part of networking. You meet many more people when you smile and say hello than you do by looking down at the ground.

A WORD TO THE WISE

If you suffer from physical problems that prevent you from getting out, it will be more challenging for you to make connections. Don't discount the effectiveness of telephone calls, and don't overlook the Internet as a means to communicate.

IT'S QUIZ TIME!

Here's a short self-assessment exercise to determine where you fall on the sociability continuum. Choose the response (a, b, or c) that best describes your reaction to the given situation.

1. You and your wife are attending a big open house at the home of one of your wife's coworkers. Your wife knows some of the people there, but you don't know a soul. What do you do?

   ___ (a) Grab a drink and make the rounds, meeting about everyone at the party by the end of the evening.

   ___ (b) Stick close to your wife and ask her to introduce you to the people she knows.

   ___ (c) Find a magazine and a quiet corner, and stay out of the way while your wife mingles.

2. You have accompanied your husband to his company's Christmas party. Dinner is over, and your husband has left the table to help set up for the office variety show. What do you do?

   ___ (a) Run up on the stage and offer to be master of ceremonies.

   ___ (b) Check out what other spouses may have been abandoned and go chat with some of them.

   ___ (c) Sit at the table by yourself and sulk because your husband left you.

3. New neighbors have just moved in across the street. What do you do?

   ___ (a) Organize a block party so they can meet everyone in the neighborhood.

   ___ (b) Make some vegetable soup or a pie and deliver it, along with your greetings and best wishes.

   ___ (c) Figure you'll meet them soon enough and go about your own business.

4. You've just heard that a coworker has had a baby. You don't know her very well, but there aren't many women in your office, and the two of you spent

a lot of time comparing notes and talking during her pregnancy. What do you do?

___ (a) Rush right over to the hospital with a huge bunch of musical balloons.

___ (b) Send a card with your best wishes and a note to call you when she feels up to having a visitor because you'd love to see her and the baby.

___ (c) Think about sending a card but then get busy and forget about it.

5. Someone in your neighborhood is trying to organize a block party, and he's put the word out that he needs some help. What do you do?

___ (a) Tell him you have lots of experience planning things like this and say you'll be more than happy to take the whole thing off his hands.

___ (b) Call him and tell him you'll be happy to help in whatever way you can.

___ (c) Don't say a word and hope he doesn't think to call you.

6. You're traveling on an airplane, and you're seated with a stranger on either side. At the end of the trip, you...

___ (a)... know your seatmates' names, ages, destinations, family backgrounds, business backgrounds, and thoughts on nuclear proliferation.

___ (b)... know where your seatmates live and where they're going.

___ (c)... have not acknowledged your seatmates.

7. Your 10-year class reunion is coming up. What do you do?

___ (a) Call the class president and volunteer to chair the committee to plan the reunion.

___ (b) Send in your reply card to say you'll be there.

___ (c) Decide you're not going because there's really nobody you want to see.

8. A new woman is hired in your office. What do you do?

___ (a) Take her on a tour of the building and introduce her to everybody, then take her out to lunch.

___ (b) Introduce yourself and tell her to let you know if there's anything she needs.

___ (c) Ignore her until someone introduces you.

9. You're invited back to your high school as a guest speaker at an awards assembly. What do you do?

___ (a) Say you'll be more than happy to do it and immediately start working on your speech.

___ (b) Agree to do it but suffer much trepidation and anxiety before the day of the assembly.

___ (c) Refuse the invitation because you know you could never stand in front of a group and make a speech.

10. A young person asks you to help him find a summer job. What do you do?

___ (a) Get on the phone and call everybody you know who might be able to help.

___ (b) Help him check the classified ads to see what's available.

___ (c) Tell him you're too busy to help at this time.

How Did You Do?

If most of your answers were (a), then you are probably a very outgoing, sociable person who looks for and takes advantage of networking opportunities. The only thing you'll need to watch for is overdoing it, that is, appearing to be a busybody who needs to be in control all the time.

If most of your answers were (b), then you fall in about the middle of the sociability continuum. You'll have to be careful that you don't overlook opportunities to connect and expand you network.

If most of your answers were (c), then you'll need to work hard on your social skills. Good networkers don't keep to themselves and aren't reluctant to get involved.

I'D LIKE YOU TO MEET...

Karen Kelly, the New York editorial director of Daybreak Books, is an outgoing, sociable person and a great networker. Every now and then, though, she goes into what she calls hibernation mode. "I do retreat a lot of times," she admits. "It's a natural rhythm. Sometimes I really want to be around a lot of people, and other times I want to hibernate and not see anybody."

Even when she's in her hibernation mode, however, Karen recognizes the value of networking. She says when she doesn't want to be around people or spend a lot of time talking to them, she'll keep in touch by writing a note or sending an e-mail. "It doesn't matter so much how you do it, as long as you stay in touch," she says.

Make Yourself Useful

Your network will never stop growing if you make yourself necessary to others. As long as people need you, you'll have a special spot in their card files.

How do you become necessary? Volunteer to do things. Serve on committees. Become known as someone who can be counted on to get things done. Once you do that, your phone will never stop ringing, and you'll meet all sorts of people while you're being useful. Consider for a moment the rewards of volunteerism.

I've served for a couple of years as chairwoman of the public relations committee for a chef's auction to benefit my community's chapter of the March of Dimes. The popular event—a combined food festival and auction—is held at a local country club. My involvement in the event requires attending about six meetings and arranging for newspaper and television coverage of the event. It takes some time, but the payoff is well worth the effort. Volunteering for this job has given me all kinds of opportunities to meet and network with a lot of interesting people.

I've gotten to know all the other volunteers, who represent a variety of businesses and other organizations; March of Dimes board and staff members; a couple dozen of the area's top chefs; and people associated with the country club at which the event is held. Plus, as a committee member, I'm in a good position to meet people at the event.

Granted, making yourself needed requires a commitment of time and energy on your part, but networking is reciprocal. Those that give, receive.

Red, Yellow, Black, and White

The best networks are diverse networks. They are made up of people of different races, religions, ages, and economic groups who have varied interests.

Think about people who have helped you over the years—a pretty mixed group, right? People from different backgrounds can expose you to new experiences and introduce you to people you might not ordinarily meet. Think of the opportunities that might pop up if you get to be good friends with a foreign exchange student—someone to visit in Sweden, Cameroon, or New Zealand, for example.

Make a point of diversifying your network. Join some groups where people of different backgrounds belong. Attend events dealing with cultural or foreign issues at a local university, and see who you meet.

If everyone in your network is just like you, it will be a pretty limited—and limiting—group.

Don't Get Too Comfortable

A great way to make sure your network never stops growing is to extend your range of interests and activities. Spending time with the same old group of friends is nice, but that's not going to put new names in your card file.

Think about what you do in a typical day. If every day you drive to work, pop over to the gym afterward, then pick up some dinner at the Golden Chopsticks or the Chicken Shack on your way home, then your networking opportunities are limited to those experiences.

Now consider the possibilities if after work you join the local bicycling club for a ride, go to the meeting of that professional women's group you've been wanting to check out, or play a set at the tennis club. What if you join a supper club, your church choir, a rock climbing group, a stamp collecting club, the Rotary club, or your township's beautification committee?

As you expand your interests and activities, you'll meet more people who can become part of your network. You'll also become a more interesting and knowledgeable person—the kind of person that others want in their networks.

There are big dividends for those who break out of their comfort zones and expand their interests and their networks.

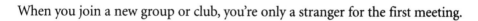

A WORD TO THE WISE

When you join a new group or club, you're only a stranger for the first meeting.

Go For It

Think of somebody famous you'd really like to meet. Maybe you've just read a piece about newswoman Cokie Roberts and you think she sounds like the most interesting person, or maybe you've always considered Barbra Streisand a personal hero. Go ahead and take a shot—write her a letter. Tell her that you've always admired her. Ask her how she maintains her incredible energy level or her idealism after all these years. You might not get an answer, but maybe you will.

Karen Kelly is a great advocate of chance-taking, and she practices what she preaches. She once saw Bob Guccione, Jr., the founder of *Spin* magazine, on a television show. She listened to what he had to say and liked it, so she wrote him a letter saying that she had enjoyed the show and his comments.

The day after Guccione got the letter, he called Karen. They've since become friends, and Karen was offered—but declined—the opportunity to work for him.

"If you're writing a letter to someone that's complimentary, and you're not asking for anything, what can you possibly lose?" she says. "The worst that will happen is that you won't get an answer. So what?"

IT'S UP TO YOU

There are lots of ways to make sure your network never stops expanding, but it's up to you to put them into action. Nobody can maintain your network for you; it requires the personal touch.

Only you will network exactly the way you do. The longer you network, the more creative you'll become about how to expand your group of contacts. You'll become more aware of the people you meet and more attuned to making them part of your network.

Networking Notes

- If you meet new people on a regular basis, there's no reason for your network to ever stop growing.
- If you're not in a position to meet new people regularly, you'll have to be creative in finding ways to keep expanding your network.
- Be sociable and friendly to make yourself open to opportunities that will allow you to expand your network.
- Keep your network growing by volunteering to serve on a committee or joining a civic, professional, or community group.
- Remember that schools—your own or your kids'—are great places to meet people you can add to your network.
- To expand its reach, keep your network diverse.
- Vary your routine to give you more opportunities to meet people.
- If you want to meet someone, even someone famous, go ahead and write a letter. You have nothing to lose.

CHAPTER | 15

DON'T UNDERESTIMATE THE VALUE OF PERIODICALS AND THE INTERNET

Y ou've learned about ways to network and make contacts with other people—phone calls, notes, letters, and face-to-face meetings. You now have dozens of ideas for meeting people who might become part of your network and for developing relationships with those people. It would be remiss, however, to not explore some other important networking methods—specifically, business journals, trade magazines, and the Internet.

PERIODICALS

You can never have too much information. The broader your base of information, the better off you'll be. Did you ever notice that an interesting, well-informed person will say something like, "Oh yes, I read about that in last week's issue of *Time*," "There was a piece about that in *Vanity Fair* last month," or, "*Forbes* did an analysis on that subject." Well-informed people read a variety of publications that deal with a wide range of topics. These people can talk about almost anything.

I'm not saying you should go out and buy every magazine off the rack. It's not a bad idea, however, to go to a bookstore or magazine shop and take a good look at the periodicals that are available. You might be surprised by the variety of specialty magazines, and you might just learn something about a particular industry or area that pertains to your job search.

Some trade publications that you probably didn't realize exist include

- *Glass Magazine*, for the architectural glass industry
- *The Paint Dealer*, for the retail paint market
- *National Home Center News*, for the retail home improvement market
- *Mini-Storage Messenger*, for the self-storage industry
- *The Preacher's Magazine*, for ministers
- *Ornamental Outlook*, for commercial growers of ornamental plants in Florida
- *Shoe Retailing Today*, for the footwear and accessory industry
- *Southern Lumberman*, for the sawmill industry

There are tons of trade magazines, but they aren't always easy to get your hands on. Your library might have some, but probably not an extensive collection. It may have an industry list of trade publications instead. If you can obtain this list, you can call the publication you're interested in and see what you have to do to get a copy. Many trade publications are listed in online databases, too.

General business periodicals such as *Forbes*, the *Wall Street Journal*, *Barrons*, and *Business Week* are excellent for getting a general feel for the job market. You can learn about important business and economic trends, expansion or downsizing of major companies, and key people in a particular industry. You also can get tips on job hunting and career advancement. To learn specifically about your field and jobs available in it, you should check out a trade publication.

SURFIN' THE WEB

The Internet is an exciting new means of communicating and obtaining information that has opened up doors we never even knew were there. It is a worldwide system of computer networks that link together all kinds of businesses, universities, government agencies, and individuals.

F.Y.I.

I once worked for a small company that insured pest control operators—you know, the guys who come to your house or office when you have an infestation of ants, roaches, bees, or some other creepy-crawlies. I was surprised to learn that there are three national magazines for the pest control industry, each of which contained a classified section that listed job and business opportunities. About 40 states have pest control organizations that publish newsletters, including job listings. Many states also have regional organizations, some of which also have newsletters.

My point is that there are thousands of publications that we'll never know about unless we really look.

In a very short time, the Internet has become a technological tool that many people couldn't live without. We can zap messages back and forth to people across the country and around the world. We can access information about topics we never knew existed and research virtually any subject from our desktops. The Internet also is quickly becoming an indispensable tool for job hunting.

An article in the March 1998 issue of *Fortune* magazine was entitled "Changing Jobs? Try the Net. The Internet is a far more powerful job-search tool than it was just months ago. Now you can't ignore it." It's a long title for a magazine piece, but a convincing bit of advertising for the value of the Internet.

The Internet is useful not only for searching for a job but also for obtaining information and advice about nearly every aspect of career preparation, change, and advancement. Some job-related topics and services that you'll find online include

- Self-assessment tests to determine the kind of job you should be looking for
- Career counseling to determine whether you'll be successful and happy in the job you've chosen
- The perfect résumé (how to write it yourself or hire someone online to write it for you)
- Tips for having a perfect interview (you can even participate in a virtual interview)
- How to negotiate the salary you want
- Salary comparisons and the cost of living in different states and regions
- International employment opportunities

- Special information just for recent college grads
- Information about specific companies or industries

In addition, many newspapers and periodicals have online, or electronic, versions on the Web—*USA Today, Forbes, Time, Fortune, Life, Money,* and *Business Week,* for example. Some post the entire issue same as the print publication; others post only cover stories or a few features of interest. Access may be free, subject to a subscription fee, or a combination of both. Search the Internet for the home pages of your favorite publications and see what they have to offer.

F.Y.I.

If you don't know the Web site address (also called a URL) for your favorite publication, you can do one of several things: check the print publication for the URL of its home page, use one of the online services to search for the URL by publication name, or venture a guess.

I usually guess. Most online magazines use the same kind of format: www.magazinename.com (with no internal spaces and no end period). So, by substituting the name of the magazine you want to find, you have a pretty good chance of finding it. I found the Business Week Online site, for example, by simply typing http://www.businessweek.com in the "Go to" field on my Internet browser, hitting Enter, and voilà.

Getting Online

How do you begin to use the Internet for networking purposes? That's a really good question. All kinds of books, manuals, and articles have been written to teach you how to use the Internet, and some people think they're must-reads before you get online. Others claim that the best way to master the Net is to dive right in and explore it on your own.

Either way, you'll have to set some time aside to learn to "surf." It can take forever to plod through a how-to manual, and anyone who's ever logged onto the Internet knows that the 20 minutes you give yourself to browse turns into 2½ hours before you know it.

Internet Service Providers

When you hear people talking about America Online, CompuServe, or Prodigy, they're not talking about the Internet, exactly (even though some people use the terms synonymously). The Internet is just out there. It's a vast, practically unimaginable pool of information, opportunities, and junk. Nobody owns the Internet, and nobody operates it.

These companies are Internet service providers (ISPs)—they provide access to the Internet, along with other services such as the latest news, entertainment, games, sites for kids, financial reports, access to periodicals, online shopping, and more. They also have mail servers, which allow you to send and receive electronic mail (e-mail). These companies charge users a monthly fee that varies according to the service plan the user chooses (usually based on a number of online hours).

If you choose America Online (AOL) as your ISP, the company will provide software for you to load onto your computer. You'll need a modem, a device that allows you to transfer information via your phone line to and from your computer. After you load your AOL software and follow the step-by-step instructions, you're ready to go. Every time you log onto your computer, an AOL icon will appear on your screen, giving you online access to more information than a human being can hope to process.

AOL provides a list of Web "channels" that break down the Internet into general categories, allowing you to more easily find what you need. The main AOL channels are Travel, Sports, Computing, Research, Lifestyles, WorkPlace, Health, Families, Entertainment, Personal Finance, Shopping, News, Interests, International, Local, and Kids Only.

If you click on "WorkPlace," for example, you'll see a submenu of what's available. Some of your choices are Job Postings, Your Health at Work, Rules and Regulations, Humor, and Professional Resources. When you click on one of these categories, you will get a list of Web sites dealing with that topic. "Job Postings" gave me a list of many related Web sites:

- **The Monster Board** (http://www.aboutwork.monster.com) lists more than 25,000 jobs by category and location; offers a place to post your résumé; and features information about topics including résumés, interviews, and pay scales.
- **CareerPath.com** (http://www.careerpath.com) lists more than 250,000 job listings from 60+ major metropolitan newspapers and offers a place to post your résumé.
- **Career Mosaic** (http://www.careermosaic.com) lists jobs and gives you access to all sorts of topics concerning job hunts, networking, and other job-related topics. It also gives you access to discussion groups.

- **AOL Classifieds** (http://dynamic.aol.com) is an online job-posting site for jobs nationwide.

When I clicked on "Humor," I found these among the many Web sites listed:

- **Dilbert** (http://www.unitedmedia.com/comics/dilbert), the online version of the popular comic strip.
- **For Web Addicts** (http://www.donsbosspage.com) provides a link that you click on when your boss walks by; it will replace whatever is on your computer screen with some official looking "work."
- **My Boss** (http://www.myboss.com) is a site where workers can exchange horror stories and vote for worst boss.

An alternative to using AOL's Web channels is to use AOL Net Find. You type in some key words to get a list of sites on the Internet that might apply to your search. Once you're actually connected to the Internet, you can access other search sites, too, such as Yahoo, AltaVista, and Lycos. Like the AOL search engine, they help narrow your search for particular Internet sites.

The main hurdle to overcome when you're just starting to use the Internet is intimidation. There's so much information and so many places to look. The best advice is to ask someone who knows their way around the Net to walk you through the basics the first few times you use it. After that, have fun with it, and be creative with how to use all the information you'll get.

A WORD TO THE WISE

If you are shopping for a modem, remember that faster is better. The faster your modem is, the faster you'll be able to send and receive messages and get information onto your screen. If you've ever worked with a very slow modem, you know how frustrating it can be to sit there and wait, and wait, and wait....

You will pay more for a faster modem, but it's advisable to get the fastest one you can afford. The time you save will be worth it.

Newsgroups and Virtual Job Fairs

Newsgroups, discussion groups, and chat groups are online networking centers that can be very helpful. You can access them through sites such as Monster or

Career Mosaic or try Deja News (http://www.dejanews.com), a search engine especially designed to find newsgroups and discussion groups.

People who are looking for particular jobs use these groups, as do employers looking for employees. Different groups discuss topics as diverse as

- mentoring,
- working from home,
- downsizing,
- early retirement,
- labor unions,
- power naps,
- going back to school, and
- taking daughters to work.

Some of these groups are nothing more than chat rooms where disgruntled workers complain about their bosses or how they're underpaid. The good newsgroups, though, can be very useful, because employers use them to find potential job candidates.

Another online networking tool is virtual job fairs. Although these sites have been criticized as being no more than glorified job posting boards, they provide a good idea of what jobs are available and are helpful to employers because they allow them to screen potential candidates.

Some sites claim to be able to arrange live job interviews, but most interaction is not done in real time. Some sites charge for complete access. If you want to check some out, try these:

- **The Virtual Recruiting Network** (http.//aniamag.com/infoage/virtual) features prearranged, live job interviews and global job fairs.
- **BSA Career Mart** (http://www.careermart.com) allows job hunters to browse job listings, view the home pages of various companies, and job search by region or company.
- **Virtual Job Fair** (http://www.abcompass.com) features more than 15,000 job opportunities from about 500 companies as well as about 15,000 searchable résumés.
- **Virtual Career Fair** (http://www.cweb.com/fair) offers information on jobs in many fields.

BE CAREFUL!

If you're going to use newsgroups to try to find a job, it's very important to use the correct terminology to describe your skills and the jobs you're looking for. Prospective online employers are tough on job hunters who use incorrect terms.

If you intend to join a discussion group, read the suggestions or FAQ (answers to frequently-asked questions) provided at the site so you'll know what you're talking about and how to say it without offending anyone. Or, practice in another discussion site, such as one dealing with a hobby, until you get the hang of it.

Posting Your Résumé

There are some things to keep in mind if you decide to post your résumé with a job board on the Internet. Most sites will let you post a résumé for free, passing on the cost to companies and recruiters, who pay for their searches.

Also, before you post your résumé, make sure that the site will let you edit it. If you can't retrieve it, then you won't be able to refine it or add something new when you think it's necessary.

A word of caution about posting your résumé on the Net: Once you do, it's out there, fair game. That means that anyone—including your boss and everyone else—can see it. The Internet is a big place, but it's always possible that somebody might see your résumé who you would rather not.

One alternative to throwing your résumé onto a job board and waiting for a bite is to hire what's called an intelligent agent. This agent is actually a program to which you enter information such as the kind of job you want, where you want to work, your desired salary, and other preferences. When an applicable job pops up at the Web site on which you've filed the information, you are notified by e-mail. This approach allows you to be in charge of who gets your résumé. A couple of sites that offer the intelligent agent feature are CareerBuilder (http://www.careerbuilder.com) and Nation Job Network (http://www.nationjob.com).

Getting the Inside Scoop on Companies

How do you know whether you should apply for a job you see posted on the Internet? The company may be in financial trouble or have a history of layoffs and downsizing, but that information is not likely to be posted at the company's home page. Most company Web sites are essentially advertisements for which the company has paid big bucks. You're not going to find any dirty laundry there.

What you won't find on a company's home page you might find elsewhere on the Internet. Annual reports, company profiles, lists of officers, stock charts, and the like are available at some sites. You might even find recent articles online that were written about the company. Two such sites are

- **Hoover's** (http://www.hoovers.com), which offers free information about businesses and links to other helpful sites, and
- **The United States Securities and Exchange Commission** (http://www.sec.gov), which posts annual reports online.

F.Y.I.

The TWA Web site (http://www.TWA.com) contains a feature called "Significant Dates in TWA History." These dates include when in-flight movies were added, no-smoking sections were first offered, Pope Paul VI flew TWA from New York to Rome, the Constellation Club opened at Kennedy Airport in New York, and a comfort class was inaugurated.

Nowhere, however, is the 1996 crash of Flight 800 off of Long Island mentioned. If that's not a significant event in TWA's history, I don't know what is. It simply is a topic that TWA does not care to publicize on its Web site.

Pros and Cons of Using the Internet to Find a Job

Using the Internet for your job search has many advantages. You can find information on almost every aspect of job hunting and browse postings of thousands of available jobs. But there are some potential downsides, as well: isolation and lack of privacy.

The Good Stuff

Carol Turkington is a writer in Morgantown, Pennsylvania. She has found several writing jobs online and has used the Internet to locate doctors, psychologists, and other experts to work with her on books or articles.

One great benefit of the Internet, Carol says, is timeliness. Newsletters publish job listings on their publication dates, but jobs can be posted on the Internet as they become available and removed as they are filled. "Lots of writer organizations have job lines," she explains. "The problem with many of them is if you only get the newsletter once a month, some of the jobs may have been filled by the time the newsletter comes out. With the associations now going online, their job lines are now much more up to date, and there's a better chance of actually getting a job."

Your job hunt can be conducted in the comfort and privacy of your own home—in your pajamas, if you'd like. You can create and fine-tune a résumé, participate in a job interview, and take a personality test to find out what jobs suit you; you can even research companies, salaries, and the availability of jobs in different locations. All that, just by clicking some keys and pushing some buttons. You never even have to say a word.

The Bad Stuff

The big disadvantage of using the Internet to conduct your job search is that it's very easy to become isolated if you don't use any other sources or methods. Sure, it's easy to sit at your desk and read a computer screen—it's *too* easy.

When you hunt for jobs online, you're not practicing the skills you'll need to be successful in the workplace. You're not practicing how you present yourself to others or noticing whether your shoes are polished for a job interview.

Although online networking and job postings can be useful, they can't replace good old-fashioned face-to-face networking. Interacting with someone on the Internet is very different from meeting someone in person; it doesn't require the same social skills. Make sure that the time you spend networking on the Internet doesn't infringe on the time you spend making personal contacts and connections.

More Useful Internet Sites

Here are some Web sites related to networking, work, and job listings:

- *CareerXroads* (http://www.careerroads.com) is a book by Mark Mehler and Gerry Crispin that lists the 500 best sites for finding job listings, résumé tips, and more. The book can be bought ($22.95) in bookstores, via the Web site, or by phone at 732-821-6652.
- **Online Career Center** (http://www.occ.com) is a large site similar to Monster and Career Mosaic.
- **JobSmart** (http://www.jobsmart.org) offers salary surveys for various industries.

- **Netshare, Inc.** (http://www.netshare.com) offers access to exclusive listings of jobs with salaries of $70,000 and up.
- **About Work** (http://www.aboutwork.com) posts information about a wide variety of work- and networking-related topics.
- **The Student Center** (http://www.studentcenter.com) specializes in information about résumés and interviews for new and soon-to-be college graduates.
- **College Grads** (http://www.collegegrad.com) is another site specializing in information for new and soon-to-be college graduates.
- **The Business Channel** (http://www.infoseek.com) offers all kinds of business news, including information about stocks and where to find the best jobs.
- **Career Planning/Competency Model** (http://www.bgsu.edu/offices/careers/process/exercise.html) provides an online simulated interview and other features.
- **Career City** (http://www.careercity.com) tells you how to negotiate for the best salary.

GET TO IT!

Do you feel ready to add some less conventional sources to your job search? Head to your local library to check out the periodicals section, or jump on the Net and find yourself a job. You have plenty of places to start.

The Internet will become increasingly important as more and more people use it. By all means, use the Internet as a tool for networking—just not your only tool.

Networking Notes

- Check out business journals and trade magazines as possible sources for connections.
- The Internet is becoming an increasingly important tool for job hunting.
- You can access the Internet via many companies, which offer different services at a range of prices. Find out what's available before you choose.
- The Internet offers sites about writing résumés, conducting job interviews, negotiating salaries, and many other relevant topics.
- On the Internet you can post your résumé, check job listings, and find out about a company that interests you.
- Newsgroups, or discussion groups, can be good networking vehicles. Learn the lingo before you jump in.
- Don't let the Internet become your only networking tool. It can be isolating and actually hinder your networking efforts.

CHAPTER | 16

IT'S A DANGEROUS WORLD— NETWORK IT!

"My mother groan'd! my father wept. Into the dangerous world I leapt . . ."

Poet William Blake leapt into a dangerous world in 1757 and wrote the verse above around 1800. In some ways, the world is safer than it was then: Fewer mothers and children die during child-birth. Fewer children die of early-childhood diseases. Fewer people starve because uncontrolled insects ruined a year's crop. In other ways, though, the world is at least as dangerous now as it was in Blake's day.

We can't keep ourselves or our families completely safe all the time. Writers have made the best-seller lists advising people how to survive tragedy and persevere through times of strife. Our homes and businesses are armed with smoke detectors, fire extinguishers, carbon monoxide detectors, radon sensors, and security alarms. We are warned daily of perils such as strangers with ill intent, deer ticks, pit bulls, contaminated drinking water, and cancer-causing agents in our food.

Business owners and employees have additional worries, such as low-priced foreign labor, mergers, quality control, and downsizing.

With all these problems and dangers lurking in every corner, one thing is very good to know: You have a network to fall back on—or at least you have a good start on a network. An effective network can help you survive about any kind of crisis that comes along by minimizing damage and maximizing healing. You just have to know how to use it.

About how many names do you have in your card file or notebook by now— 50? 100? 200? Relax—nobody expects you to have anywhere near that many names. Regardless of how many names there are, you always should

- add new people to your network,
- find new ways to use your network, and
- nurture and maintain the network you have.

You learned about adding people to your network in Chapters 11 and 14, and we'll talk more about maintaining your network in later chapters. So for now, we'll discuss the second "should." You've built your network for the mutual benefit of you and the people in it. To leave a network sit untapped makes no sense.

Seasoned networkers cite situations that would have ruined them and their businesses without people in their networks to support them. Novice networkers say that through networking, they landed their first jobs, which put them on a successful career track. Let's look at some possible situations in which you'll use your network and ways that your network will be there for you.

F.Y.I.

Author and networker Harvey Mackay revealed during an interview that he has about 6,500 names in his card file. However, he admits that 80 percent of all his networking is with about 20 percent of those people.

"NOT ME" SYNDROME

Deep down, most of us think that the bad things in life will pass us over and go on to the next guy. It's a natural tendency and most likely for the best. You probably don't wake up in the morning and think that today you will

- lose your job after a hostile takeover,
- develop an incurable disease,

- lose every dollar you have in the stock market,
- get in a car crash on your way to work,
- fall down the steps and break your leg,
- come home from work and find your house burned to the ground,
- say something that terribly offends your boss and be fired, or
- be killed instantly when a meteorite crashes into your house.

Some people, unfortunately, suffer from constant dread and anxiety that something terrible will happen. Although it's unlikely that all these things will happen to any one person, reality tells us that *some* bad things happen to everyone. In some respects, Blake was right. It *is* a dangerous world in which scary things happen.

What Happened to My Job?

I had been working as a reporter for only one or two years when the family company that owned our newspaper combined the morning and afternoon staffs, which resulted in a lot of layoffs. This was a mid-sized paper where people had made careers. Many of the people who lost their jobs that day had worked for the company for 20 years or longer. In those days we didn't use the term "downsizing"; it was just a dark, quiet, and somber day.

It was a difficult time for both those who lost their jobs and those who were left. There was a lot of anger, bitterness, and tears—as well as secret relief among those of us still employed. Some of the people who had been let go found new jobs almost immediately at another paper or in public relations or another field. Others floundered around, working here and there, always waiting for something to come along.

Looking back on that experience, I can clearly see what it was that determined how these people bounced back—or didn't—after losing their jobs. It was their networks, or lack thereof.

Newspaper work is ideal for building a large, healthy network. You meet lots of people because you're always out covering a meeting or tracking down some sort of news (reporters rarely get good stories from sitting in the office). If you have a regular beat, you get to know people well because you see them all the time. You also get to know high-profile, well-connected people because those are the people making the news.

During my 10-year newspaper experience, I got to know politicians, police officers, university professors and administrators, firefighters, business owners, lawyers, doctors and others in the medical profession, homeless people, single moms raising kids in housing projects, engineers, drug addicts, recovered addicts, athletes, autistic kids, sick kids, municipal officials, school board members, refugees, artists, musicians, teachers, and trash collectors. It was a networker's dream!

For whatever reasons, some reporters don't connect—not with each other or with the people they meet on the job. They get the information they need, write a story, go home, and do it all again the next day. The do their jobs, but they're no more involved with them than a worker on a production line might be. These kinds of people flounder when laid off from their jobs. They don't know who to see to get some ideas for other employment. They withdraw from the people they knew and suffer alone, tending to their bruised egos.

The others, though, used every connection they had made while working to find out what was happening. Those people ended up working in the public relations departments of hospitals or colleges, or as press liaisons for state representatives. The people who rebounded quickly and landed on their feet weren't necessarily smarter or better qualified than their colleagues; they simply knew what had to be done.

JOB LOSS AND BEYOND

Losing your job is right up there among life's most stressful experiences. Other things test the stuff we're made of, too. If you play your cards right, your network will come through for you.

Dan's Story

In 1980, Dan and Gina Kruse had just moved to Reading, Pennsylvania, with their two daughters. Gina's parents lived near Reading, and the young couple decided to bring their family and look for work there. Dan was hoping to get into the audio-visual production business but didn't know how to get started. To support his family, he was doing odd jobs, taking whatever work he could get.

A friend of Gina's parents gave Dan the name of a man who worked at Armstrong World Industries, a large home product manufacturer in Lancaster. Dan started networking. He called the man to whom he'd been referred, even though he had never met or spoken to him. That person referred Dan to the head of Armstrong's audio-visual department, and Dan called him.

Although Dan had absolutely no experience in audiovisual work, he managed to impress the head of the department enough to land a small temporary assignment. Dan worked diligently, learning all he could as he went along. While working at Armstrong, he noticed a piece of letterhead of a nearby film production company lying on a desk. He inquired about the firm and found out it did a lot of work for Armstrong. He asked the head of the audiovisual department for a contact there and was given the name of the president.

Dan called the president of the film production company and mentioned he was doing some work for Armstrong. The president of the film production company said he didn't have any openings at that time but would be interested in meeting Dan anyway.

So, Dan met the president, who said he'd keep him in mind should any jobs open within the company. Somewhat discouraged, Dan took a job as a copywriter/production manager for a Reading radio station, even though it wasn't what he really wanted to do.

A full year later, the president of the film production company called and told Dan he had a job opening and asked whether Dan would be interested in meeting about it. Would he! Dan interviewed for, was offered, and accepted the job.

Dan turned out to be a natural. He went on to found his own company and then served as vice president of a large communications firm.

And the Secret to Dan's Success Is...

Dan's ability to network and his tenacity and determination clearly are the factors that launched his successful 15-year career in the audiovisual field. Had he been reluctant to initiate and follow up on leads, he might still be working at the radio station.

Linda's Story

Linda had a job editing medical journals in Baltimore, Maryland, when she met her future husband. Bill was British, and when he and Linda got married, she moved with him to Scotland and then to the Netherlands, where he had been transferred for his work.

Linda got another editing job and worked until she and Bill had their first child. A second baby came less than two years later, and Linda put her career on hold while she raised two children in a foreign country, with no family and few close friends around.

Later, Linda and Bill began having marital problems, and it became clear that they weren't going to resolve them. The couple divorced, and Linda's lawyer advised her that because she was no longer married to someone who was permitted to live in The Netherlands, she would have to leave the country. As difficult as it was, Linda packed up the children and moved back to the town where she had grown up. She lived with her parents for a while and then found an apartment for her and the kids.

Bill was not dependable with his support payments; the matter of support payments was complicated because he was in another country. She had no savings, because she hadn't worked since her first child was born. Things were getting desperate. Linda knew she needed to get a job, but she had to consider several factors. Most important, neither of her children was in school yet, so they'd have to be cared for while she was at work. She was reluctant to leave them to go to work—they had just lost the company of their father and had been moved from their home and to completely different surroundings. What to do?

Linda tried to think who could help. She remembered that her friend Kathy, with whom she had worked in Baltimore, still worked for the Baltimore firm even though she had moved to Florida. Would it be possible for her, too, to work for the firm without being in Baltimore?

Linda and Kathy had kept in touch, so Linda picked up the phone. Kathy was editing medical journals from her home. She gave Linda the name of the person to call at the Baltimore firm and made Linda promise to keep in touch.

Four years later, Linda is still working from home while her children go to school. It's not a perfect situation—her kids complain that she doesn't spend enough time with them, and she's not making as much money as she could be if she were using her science background—but she's at home to see her kids off to school in the morning and to meet them when they get off the bus in the afternoon. Those are the things that matter most to Linda.

Linda and Kathy talk regularly, and Linda often expresses her thanks for her friend's help.

And the Secret to Linda's Success Is...

If Linda hadn't networked with Kathy and gotten back in touch with the Baltimore firm, she believes she would have had to get a job that would have taken her away from her children when they most needed her. She says she never realized how important networking was before that point.

Arnie's Story

Arnie is one of those guys who loves to be involved. He's active in his community and knows just about everybody. He's the kind of guy who loves to help people and the guy that people call when they need some information. In other words, Arnie is a natural networker.

After serving for about four years on his township's board of commissioners—two years as chairman—Arnie decided not to run for reelection. He really liked it, but there were a lot of internal hassles and some nasty politics going on, and those weren't his bag. Instead, he ran for and was easily elected to his district's school board.

Serving on committees and listening to constituents' concerns, Arnie had a great time on the school board. He didn't mind getting phone calls at home. When Arnie said he would help someone, he always did.

Then, completely unexpectedly, Arnie, a state employee, was in big trouble.

As helpful as he'd been to a lot of people over the years, Arnie had rubbed some folks the wrong way. He's passed it off as the price of playing politics: You can't please everybody. Some people held him personally responsible for the township tax hike five years ago, and one person thought he should have been able get his kid off the hook when he was caught stealing from another kid's locker last year.

Arnie was never positive who called the state office where he works, but he has a pretty good idea who it was. It seems that technically, Arnie wasn't permitted to serve on a municipal or school board because he was a state employee. It was some obscure regulation that Arnie hadn't known about—but somebody else did. Somebody who apparently thought that blowing the whistle and getting Arnie fired from his job would be a good way to pay him back for whatever perceived woes Arnie had caused.

With two kids in college, Arnie was terrified at the thought of losing his job. He didn't know what to do, so he called his long-time lawyer, who was also a good friend. He also happened to owe Arnie a favor or two.

Yes, the lawyer confirmed, this situation could mean big trouble for Arnie. Don't worry, though, he said, he'd figure out a way to take care of it.

The lawyer called in a couple of favors on Arnie's behalf, and the problem went away after Arnie quickly and quietly resigned from the school board. Although he was disappointed that his community service has been thwarted, Arnie is thankful that he still has his job.

And the Secret to Arnie's Success Is...

Arnie's years of networking paid off when he most needed it. Keeping up connections and doing favors when you can often will pay off with big dividends. Arnie still works for the state but is looking forward to retiring—with his pension.

Tom's Story

When Tom heard his boss was going to be in Chicago on business, something clicked in his head. He had a friend in Chicago who, on several occasions, had mentioned that there was a great Indian restaurant near his apartment. Tom (and everyone else in the office) knew about the boss's passion for Indian food and that he was always on the lookout for good restaurants.

Tom got on the phone with his buddy and got not only the name and phone number for the extremely popular restaurant but also a reservation for his boss. It seems his friend was a very good customer and was able to secure a reservation, whereas an out-of-towner wouldn't have had a chance.

This bit of networking did more to impress Tom's boss than any of the best-prepared reports, and all it took was a 10-minute phone call.

And the Secret to Tom's Success Is...

Call it what you will, but that little bit of networking may have made a significant difference in Tom's career. Tom's boss, no doubt, will remember his efforts. If it comes down to Tom and another employee being evenly matched and vying for an advancement, Tom's networking efforts on behalf of his boss might pay off, big time.

Networking Notes

- Always be alert to ways that your network can work for you.
- People who rebound quickly after losing jobs probably are well connected and using their networks.
- Networking is not always easy or convenient, but when you need help, you have to reach out.
- Sometimes using your network requires ingenuity and tenaciousness, but the payoff is worth the trouble.
- When things get bad, you'd better have a network to fall back on.
- Your network can give you hope and offer possibilities when you feel you're out of options.
- Your network is also there for you to use to help others.

CHAPTER | 17

NETWORKING BEYOND "9 TO 5"

We've been talking about networking primarily as it applies to careers, but if you think about it, you'll realize that you network all the time. Networking—that is, being able to locate a person who can help you in a particular situation, with the understanding that the person may someday call on you for help—covers an array of situations and schedules.

Do you ever call a friend to see what she's wearing to the party, to ask if she can drop your kids off at home after choir practice, or to ask where she got that fabulous French bread she served at her last dinner party? That's networking. Have you ever run into someone you used to work with and proceeded to fill each other in on all the people you still keep in touch with? That's networking, too. "I think we network all the time," said Linda E., corporate human resources administrator for a large retail chain. "I network constantly for my work, but I do a lot of personal networking, as well. I think it's just human nature."

Every time you organize a car pool, a babysitting exchange, or a group of volunteers for your school's fund-raiser, you're networking. If you've ever called a friend to find out the name of a favorite restaurant or the best place to have your shoes repaired, then you've tapped into your network.

NEW IN TOWN

Susan's Story

Susan Larson Williams had networking on her mind when she and her family moved from Greensboro, North Carolina, to Reading, Pennsylvania, in 1996. It wasn't to help her find a job—she had already done that. She had landed and was starting a job as vice president for human resources at VF Corporation, a Fortune 500 company based just outside of Reading.

Moving to a new town presented challenges in addition to those connected to her new job. Susan needed to find a babysitter for her young daughter, and it couldn't be just anyone. "Of course, I wanted to find the best person I could," she explains. "My daughter was very young and we had just left everyone we knew. It was really important for me to find someone she would be comfortable with and who would give her the best possible care."

Susan had no local network in place at this time, so she set about building a new one. "I talked to everybody," she says. "I talked to spouses of people I worked with, people at the area preschools, and even my dental hygienist."

An experienced networker, Susan has no shortage of perseverance. Her efforts paid off when the wife of a fellow employee who volunteers at the local hospital gave her a name. That person wasn't available but knew of someone who might be interested. Before long, Susan had interviewed several people and found someone that both she and her daughter liked very much. The babysitter has been with them since, and it has been an extremely satisfactory arrangement. "That was some of the most important networking I ever did," Susan says.

And the Secret to Susan's Success Is...

Networking in a new place, where you don't have your accustomed group of contacts, isn't easy—but it can be done. To Susan, finding the best babysitter for her daughter was every bit as important as impressing her new boss and every bit as difficult.

Like Susan did, ask everyone you have contact with for help. You'll be surprised sometimes at where you'll find the person who has what you need.

DESPERATE TIMES, DESPERATE MEASURES

Jamie's Story

A 22-year-old friend who is a senior at a university in Pennsylvania recently told me a great networking story. Normally a diligent student, Jamie had spent too much time on extracurricular activities during the last few weeks of school. As a result, she found herself sitting in her apartment with a blank computer screen around 9 p.m. the night before her term paper was due.

Because Jamie had stayed up all night before to finish work, she wasn't in hopeless shape to write this paper. She had gathered a lot of research and could search the Internet to find more. One long, tough night and she'd have the paper ready to hand in at her 8 a.m. class. She got to work, combing through her research, looking up material on the Internet, writing, editing, rewriting, looking up more material, and spell checking. Finally, her paper was done.

Jamie was really pleased, because it was just before 4 a.m. She could print out the paper and get a couple of hours of sleep before class, or so she thought. It wasn't going to be that easy.

For reasons unknown to all, Jamie's printer would not read the print command from her computer. It sat idle, as though it had not a thing in the world to do. She had never had a problem with the printer before and didn't have the slightest idea of what to do about it. All she knew how to do with her computer was turn it on and off, save, and print.

Jamie waited for about an hour, frantically looking through printer and computer manuals. No good. It still wasn't printing, and she didn't know how to fix it. She started calling her friends. She woke up three of them, asking for ideas about how to solve this dilemma. Her friends were willing to help, but she was working on a Macintosh computer and her friends all used PCs—totally different systems.

By 5 a.m., Jamie was getting more and more frantic, thinking she had done all that work but wouldn't have the paper ready to hand in. The professor wasn't the sympathetic type who would cut her a break, either.

Jamie got an idea—a great idea, she thought. She had met a guy named Brandon at a party the weekend before. He went to a nearby university, about 20 minutes from Jamie's school. During their conversation at the party, he'd told her that he also used a Mac. They had discussed the pros and cons of Macs versus PCs and had quite a lively debate with some hard-core Windows fans.

Anyway, Jamie remembered the name of Brandon's residence hall, but she didn't know his last name or his phone number. She did, however, know a woman who lived in the same building and, fortunately, had her phone number. Taking a deep breath, she awakened yet another person. This one was only an acquaintance, not even a friend, but Jamie figured that it was time for desperate measures.

It took of lot of explaining and some pleading that bordered on begging, but Jamie finally convinced this woman to get dressed to go two floors up and wake Brandon, the guy Jamie had met at the party. All she had to do, Jamie told the woman, was give Brandon her phone number and tell him to call right away because it was an extreme emergency.

Brandon called Jamie shortly after 6 a.m., sounding not nearly as pleasant as he had been at the party. Jamie was not about to give up after doing all that work, and she convinced him to let her come to his room with a disk and print out her term paper.

Jamie got to Brandon's room just before 7 a.m., printed out the 15-page paper, and was back to school with the paper in time for her 8 a.m. class.

And the Secret to Jamie's Success Is...

Networking isn't always a piece of cake, nor is it always pretty. Jamie got the cold shoulder from more than one person that day, but she persevered.

When she called Brandon later that day to thank him, he asked if she'd go out to dinner with him. And she did.

LIFE OR DEATH

Florence's Story

Non-work-related networking can bring about results as inconsequential as a restaurant reservation or can be a quite serious matter. If you know somebody who needs a rare and serious operation, calling around to find out who is the very best doctor to do the job literally can be a matter of life and death.

My neighborhood is a good mix of people of all ages and life situations. We have widows and widowers, teenagers, working parents, empty nesters, retirees, preschoolers, babies, stay-at-home moms, and adolescents. Because people are always around, neighbors keep an eye on each other. We network with each other on behalf of neighbors, setting up meal delivery or help with chores if needed. Our neighborhood network has even saved the life of Florence, an elderly diabetic woman, on several occasions.

Florence is severely diabetic and has no relatives who live nearby. It's difficult for her to get around, and she often doesn't feel up to cooking for herself, even though it's very important that she eat healthy meals at regular intervals. To ensure that she does, the neighbors have established a network of caregivers. Some neighbors take meals, while others help with chores such as shoveling the sidewalk, picking up groceries at the store, and taking out trash.

One neighbor checks on Florence each morning, and another checks on her at night. If something seems amiss—a light not on when it should be, or a shade left open—one neighbor will call another to go over together to see if everything is okay. On three or four occasions, neighbors have found that Florence forgot or neglected to take her insulin and had gone into diabetic shock. Emergency personnel were notified immediately. Doctors told Florence that if emergency crews hadn't been summoned, she probably would have died.

And the Secret to Florence's Success Is...

Florence's neighborhood network enables her to stay in her home instead of moving to a nursing home. Her neighborhood network also may have saved her life several times.

IT'S NOT *ALL* THAT SERIOUS

On a lighter note, one of my favorite networking stories involves a friend who faced a huge crisis on her wedding day.

Leigh Anne's Story

Like all brides, Leigh Anne wanted everything to be perfect for her late-afternoon garden wedding, and it seemed that it would be. The weather was good, the flowers were beautiful, the musicians were ready, and the tent looked elegant on the wide lawn. She was about to go and check on the dresses for the flower girls when she saw the caterers coming into the yard with her wedding cake.

Leigh Anne watched as the caterers carried the top two tiers of the cake down some steps that led to the front yard, where the tent was set up. She continued to watch—with horror—as one of the caterers stumbled on the stone step, fell forward, and sent the cake flying into the nearby ivy. There was complete silence for about a full minute as everyone processed the enormity of the situation.

Finally, Leigh Anne approached the caterer very calmly and asked if she was all right. Then, she asked what they would do about the cake. The caterer, who has gone into a different business since then, was in tears. It was too late to bake another cake, she said, and she didn't know what to do.

Being a most resourceful woman and a champion networker, Leigh Anne went into the house and thought for a few minutes. Then, she called a close friend who did some catering on the side and explained the situation. Her wedding was set to start in four hours and the cake was lying in pieces in the ivy. Was there anything to be done? The friend gave Leigh Anne some names of people to call and said she'd make some calls, too. On Leigh Anne's fourth phone call, she came up a winner.

Two sisters who made wedding and birthday cakes as a side business said they could have another wedding cake done and delivered within six hours. They couldn't guarantee it would be exactly what Leigh Anne had wanted, but if she would tell them what it should look like, they would make sure it was similar to what she had ordered originally.

Leigh Anne took a deep breath. Six hours was cutting it close, she told them. Could they make it five? They'd see what they could do. She told them what she wanted and went back to her other tasks.

The cake arrived just as the ceremony ended, none of the guests were the wiser, and the wedding party had a huge laugh over the whole thing. It's become a classic story, which nicely illustrates the power of networking.

And the Secret to Leigh Anne's Success Is...

It's not a matter of life and death, but a wedding cake lying in pieces in the ivy can be a pretty serious matter, if it's yours. The more varied your network, the more options you'll have when such a crisis occurs.

GETTING WHAT YOU NEED

Charlie's Story

Charlie moved back to New Jersey from California after ending a long-term relationship. He was sad, angry, and broke.

Charlie had never been good at saving money and had lost his job as a graphics designer about three months before he moved back east. Losing his job was depressing, and the little bit of money he had in his savings account didn't last very long.

With no money, no job, and no girlfriend, Charlie knew his options were limited. He moved back to his parents' house. He lived with his parents for a few months while he started a new job, but it quickly became clear that he would not be able to bunk with his folks for very long—it just wasn't going to work out. Fortunately, Charlie was soon doing well enough to rent a place of his own, but he had nothing to put in it and couldn't afford to buy furniture yet.

Charlie gained new respect for his mother's networking skills as she started spreading the word that Charlie was home and needed furniture. Nearly every day, somebody called to report furniture that was up for grabs: Marilyn had just gotten a new sofa and loveseat and was looking for something to do with the old furniture; Catherine had decided to change her guest room over to an office and had a bedroom set to give away.

Soon, Charlie was nicely situated in a furnished apartment, compliments of his mother's networking talents.

And the Secret to Charlie's Success Is...
After being out on his own, it wasn't easy for Charlie—or his folks—to live back at home. His mother's networking skills, however, not only got Charlie some free furniture but possibly saved his relationship with his parents.

LITTLE THINGS MEAN A LOT

Sometimes we take for granted all the little things that people in our networks do for us. We tend to overlook the kindness and help we receive—and give—every day. These small acts are some of the best examples of networking.

A Day at the Beach

Imagine that you've just left home for a week at the beach. The car is packed up to the roof with beach towels, sand and water toys, suitcases, coolers, and who knows what else. There are three bikes on the roof rack, and the smell of salt air is just a few hours away.

As you cross the state line, you have a terrible thought: you think you left the garage door open. In a rush, you had run out the front door, never thinking to check the garage. You have a sick, sinking feeling in your stomach thinking about telling your family that you're going to have to turn the car around. You can hear the whining already that will come from the back seat.

Wait! Maybe you won't have to backtrack after all. Your next-door neighbors have your electric garage door opener. Maybe someone is home.

You dial your neighbor's phone number on the car phone, and she's on the line in 30 seconds. The problem has been resolved. Your neighbor had already noticed that the garage door was up and had used the opener to close it. There's no need to turn around now. You will, however, have to remember to bring your neighbor a big box of salt-water taffy from the beach.

Time To Get the Kids

Every working parent probably has a story like this one. You're getting ready to leave work, not a minute too soon. You have to pick up your kids at school. It's pouring down rain, and you don't want them to have to wait for you outside in the pick-up area.

As you're putting the last of the work you'll take home into your briefcase, your boss walks over and says he needs "a quick meeting." Your heart sinks, because there's no such thing as a "quick" meeting with this boss. You're frustrated, upset, and worried about your kids, but you don't want to tell your boss you can't meet with him. What to do?

Your friend Joanne, a stay-at-home mom, has bailed you out before when you couldn't get to the school on time. You call her, and she says she'll be glad to pick up your kids when she gets hers. Don't worry, she says, your kids can stay at her house for as long as they need to.

Whew! Another crisis averted, thanks to someone in your network.

Car Trouble

I was driving home alone one night around 11:30 p.m. after leaving the newspaper where I was working. It was storming something awful—thunder, lightning, and pouring rain.

On a dark stretch of road, my car stopped. This wasn't the first time my car had done this. My car was very temperamental, especially in the rain, but these certainly were the worst circumstances in which it had ever happened. There I was, a young woman in a broken-down car, all by myself in the middle of a thunderstorm, pulled off on the shoulder of a dark road. Not my first choice of things to do after work, around midnight, or in the rain.

I tried to think of the best thing to do. I wasn't going to get out and go anywhere; the nearest exit and telephone were a couple of miles away. I put on my four-way flashers and tried not to despair, but it was really scary! After a while, a car pulled over ahead of me. I locked my doors and waited, more frightened than ever.

The occupants of the car were a young couple driving around with a cranky baby. They agreed to give me a ride to the nearest exit. There was an all-night diner there, and I could call someone for help. But who? It was after midnight and still pouring rain.

A group of reporters I worked with unwound most nights at the bar across the street from the newspaper. I looked up the number and called. Fortunately, some of them were still there. Sure, they'd be happy to come get me and take me home. They'd even get something to eat at the all-night diner. We'd worry about the car tomorrow.

It sure is a good feeling to have people you can count on to call in the middle of a night, even in a thunderstorm. Another networking success story!

BE PREPARED

Having a network you can count on can make your life a lot easier. Whether the situation you find yourself in is serious or not-so-serious, members of your network can make it easier to handle.

Life hands us many things—some good, some bad. You can be better prepared to deal with all these things if you have a network to help you.

Networking Notes

- Some of the most important networking you'll ever do won't have anything to do with your career.
- Off-the-job networking can be as inconsequential as finding a good restaurant or as serious as saving your life.
- People in your network are generally happy to help with non-work-related issues. After all, everyone can relate to hard times or personal problems.
- Be creative when thinking of ways your network can help in situations outside of work. Having a variety of people in your network gives you more opportunities for help.
- Look for ways that you can help people in your network who are having problems before they ask for help.

CHAPTER | 18

NETWORKING IS A TWO-WAY STREET

You have learned how to determine what people can do for you in the networking game—digging into your network to find the person who can give you the information, job tip, or reference you need. You also learned that every person in your network adds some value to your network, be it information, expertise, experience, knowledge, or connections.

Networking gives you all kinds of opportunities to get help from other people. It also gives you something else that's every bit as important: the opportunity for you to help others. From the beginning of this book, you've learned that networking's dual purpose is to give and to receive. Anyone who gets into networking with a "What can I get out of this?" mentality won't be networking for very long. It is most definitely a two-way street.

One of the beauties of networking is that it greatly multiplies your strengths and compensates for your weaknesses. If you know about something important, somebody in your network will know more—and he or she will know someone who knows even more. If you need information and don't have it, somebody in your network will either have what you need or know where to get it.

Donna Fisher, a nationally known networking expert, says networking is a cooperative group effort. "I like to compare networking with the old barn-raising parties," she says, "where people came together and combined their skills and talents to get a job done in one day that would have otherwise taken one person much longer."

A WORD TO THE WISE

As a player in the networking game, you have to be ready and willing to give.

WHAT CAN I DO?

Maybe you're not the most well connected or knowledgeable person in the world or even in your office. Maybe you're not working, so you don't have an office. It doesn't matter. You always can find ways to help people in your network. Take a few minutes and think about it. Here are a few suggestions for starters.

Pass Job Leads to Others

If you're in the job market, especially if you're just starting in your career, you might wonder how you can help someone else. Being in the job market gives you access to all kinds of information, and that makes you a valuable asset to other people's networks.

If you hear about a job that sounds great, just not for you, pass along the information to a friend or acquaintance. This is the most common form of networking. Keep in mind that once you give someone a tip, that person will be inclined to do the same for you when they hear something.

Review Résumés and Cover Letters

You have a really terrific résumé, but your friend John... his résumé really could use some work. If you're in the know about writing résumés and cover letters, offer to help John redo his. He'll be at a real disadvantage when he starts looking for jobs if his résumé and cover letters are unprofessional, incomplete, or just plain unattractive.

If somebody else did your terrific résumé, give John the name of your contact.

Give Names to Employers

If you're ever in the position of being able to recommend someone for a job, you have a perfect opportunity to tip your networking favor scale to the credit side. I often am asked to do small freelance jobs. If I can't do one, I provide the names of two or three people I know who might take it. It's especially gratifying to help someone who is just getting started in a writing career and really appreciates these opportunities.

Volunteer for Informational Interviews

If you're in a career situation and hear about someone who's looking for a job in your field, volunteer to give an informational interview. Even if you have been working only a few years, you have no doubt accumulated a lot of information that you could pass along.

Sharing your attitudes about your work, how work meshes with your family and social life, your career expectations, pros and cons of the job, and so on could be very valuable to someone considering a career in your field.

Be a Mentor

A person who has been working for only three or four years is a veteran to someone who's starting out, either in a career or in the job market in general. If you know somebody just starting out, take an interest and offer some suggestions and guidance.

If a brand-new employee starts in your department, offer to show him or her the ropes—explain procedures and philosophies relating to your business or company. You never know where the people you help at the start will end up, do you?

Take a Load (of Work) off

If you're thinking about quitting time and you see your boss, in typical fashion, hand the guy at the desk next to yours a huge file with instructions to "get this done before you leave tonight," you really ought to think about sticking around.

Your office mate is swamped. He knows it, you know it, and he knows that you know it. Your help would, undoubtedly, be much appreciated. And who knows on whose desk the folder will end up the next time?

A WORD TO THE WISE

Don't hesitate to offer help because you think you're not qualified. Sharing any kind of experience and information can be valuable.

Help Brainstorm

Did you ever have a major project that was about due, and you just didn't know where to start? It's the sort of thing that keeps you awake at night. It might be a big report or a presentation that requires graphs and tables. Whatever the project, it nearly always helps to brainstorm with someone about it.

Be alert to these situations, and volunteer to help out. Give suggestions, or just listen. The person responsible for the project often will come up with his own ideas after talking it through with a colleague.

Listen

Sometimes, really helping someone requires nothing more than a sympathetic ear. Hearing someone out is a simple, yet often overlooked, means of helping. Someone once said that people come equipped with two ears and one mouth, and they should use them to that proportion. Words to live by.

Encourage the Discouraged

Learn to recognize when someone is having a bad day and offer a little boost. Not everyone moans and groans and kicks the water cooler, you know. Some people suffer in silence, but an attentive networker can learn to recognize the signs.

If you see someone who looks down, is unusually quiet, or seems depressed, give a kind word. You don't have to ask what's wrong or even recognize that the person looks down. Just make it known that you're around.

Give Somebody a Loan

My friend Cindy had been at home raising her kids and doing every conceivable volunteer job at their schools for 12 years. When her youngest child started first grade, she was eager to get back into her advertising career. Money was *really* tight, and she was looking forward to some office camaraderie after being at home for so long.

Cindy got her résumé in shape and fired up her old networking skills. Soon, she had interviews scheduled. The problem was, her wardrobe consisted of jeans, khakis, jerseys, and two long, flowing skirts. Nothing that would impress a prospective employer. And she didn't have a couple hundred dollars to go out and buy a great "interview suit."

Another friend, Judy, had given up her job as an office administrator in favor of doing stenciling from her home. She had a closet full of beautiful clothes, including 11 designer suits, that she'd accumulated over 15 years of office work. Judy knew of Cindy's clothing shortage and graciously invited her over to tour her closet.

Cindy and Judy are about the same size, and Cindy found not one suit but three that were perfect for impressing prospective employers. Judy threw in some blouses and even the accessories she had worn with the suits; all Cindy had to do was buy shoes. Cindy looked and felt great in Judy's clothes, and she got a job about a month after she started looking.

A WORD TO THE WISE

Don't be afraid of offending someone by offering your help. He can always say "no" if he doesn't want it.

Outside the Office

Networking outside of work is often a natural, spontaneous type of connection. We network all the time but don't think of it as such. Whatever your personal network can do for you, you can do for the other members. Don't hesitate to tap into your network to help a friend with a non-professional matter. Your life is much more than your work—and your work is much more than your job.

There are many ways that you can help others in your network, in both work-related and personal situations. If a friend is swamped with work at home, offer to drive her kid to and from soccer practice so she can work uninterrupted. If you know your colleague is burning the midnight oil at the office, stop by with a cup of coffee on your way back from the movie. Small gestures are often the most appreciated and most remembered.

I'D LIKE YOU TO MEET...

One of the most beautiful examples of personal networking I've ever heard of occurred about two years ago in a neighborhood outside of Reading, Pennsylvania.

Kathy, a woman in her 30s, was diagnosed with breast cancer. She was a stay-at-home mom with three young kids—two of them not even school age. Kathy and her husband were devastated. She was worried about her condition but even more worried about her children—Who would take care of them? How would they cope? Would her husband be able to take off work while she was hospitalized? What would happen to them if she died?

While she worried, the women in her neighborhood got busy networking. They called neighbors, members of Kathy's church, and other stay-at-home moms. In an incredibly short time, they had arranged for dinners to be cooked and dropped off, hot and ready to eat, at Kathy's house each evening.

They organized a list of child-care providers and set up a day-care schedule for Kathy's preschoolers. They arranged for teenagers to babysit at night, so Kathy's husband could go to the hospital. Some agreed to take turns cleaning Kathy's house; others would do laundry. They kept her house filled with flowers from their gardens. They called other people and asked them to send cards and to pray.

This outpouring of generosity was a model of efficiency. Kathy underwent a mastectomy, chemotherapy, and an uncertain, scary recovery. She's not out of the woods yet, but her doctors are hopeful that she'll be okay. She lives with worry every day that the cancer will return but will never forget the love and caring that these women, an integral part of her network, provided for her and her family.

Brownnoser or Savvy Networker?

One of my first jobs was in an office with an obsessive boss who worked about 19 hours a day. This guy was a classic. He'd get so caught up in what he was doing that he'd forget about meetings, miss appointments, and generally drive everybody nuts. He often would be in his office for an entire day without stopping to take a break, eat, or even get a cup of coffee.

A coworker used to occasionally pick up sandwiches and sodas for the boss when he was out to lunch. The rest of us called this guy nicknames that weren't very flattering, but looking back, I wonder. Maybe that guy was just a smart net-worker, working his way up.

WHEN SHOULD YOU HELP?

When should you help someone? The obvious answer is, "When you're asked to." The correct answer, however, is, "Before you're asked to."

Keep your eyes open for opportunities to help, and don't forget to think of them as opportunities, not obligations. Whenever you help, you set the stage for reciprocity.

WHEN SHOULD YOU *NOT* HELP?

Networking is sometimes a tricky business. I keep emphasizing how important it is to help a member of your network when the opportunity arises. Now, I'm going to tell you that there are times when you shouldn't.

Get it straight, you say? Well, there's no cut-and-dried rule for when to say "no," but sometimes you have to. Think about it.

Then, Three Years Later...

What would you say if an old friend called you, out of the blue, three years after her last contact, asking you to get her an interview with your aunt, who is an accounting supervisor for a large industry in your city?

I'm not going to tell you what to say—that's your choice. If you want to help her, go ahead. You're a nicer person than most of us. Maybe your friend has been too busy cleaning out her sock drawer to give you a call or send you a Christmas card. Yeah, right.

You would be completely justified in telling your friend to take a hike (nicely, of course). You sent Christmas cards and e-mails that went unanswered and had just about written her off. I mean, how many times should you make the effort to stay connected if the other person doesn't respond? Hey, three years is a long time to be incommunicative—no quick "how ya doing" phone call, no two-line e-mail, not even a preprinted Christmas card. And the first time you hear from her, she wants something.

If you feel like you're being used, you probably are. Follow your instincts when things like this happen because inevitably, they will.

BE CAREFUL!

No matter how angry or upset you get at somebody in your network, do everything you can to stay in control. After you cool down and take an objective look, you'll only feel foolish for having lost your temper and screamed at someone.

"One Way" Is the Wrong Way

Karen Kelly, New York editorial director for Daybreak Books, tells a story about a woman who worked in publishing but left the industry to become a headhunter. She hadn't been in her new job very long before she called Karen to ask for a favor: She wanted names of writers and editors to add to her list of prospects. Being a good networker, Karen gave her as many names as she could think of.

A while later, Karen became dissatisfied with her job and called her headhunter friend for some leads. A few days went by, then a week. She called again. Still no return call.

Several years have passed, and Karen never did hear back from that headhunter friend. If she ever does hear from her, she expects it will be for another favor. That favor, says Karen, will not be granted.

Time To Cut 'em Loose

When you have given, and given, and given to a person in your network and have got nothing in return, it might be time to remove that name from your list. "Sometimes you have to weed out your Rolodex," Karen Kelly suggests. "I do it about once a year."

Booting someone out of your network isn't a pleasant task, but Karen turns it into a positive exercise. "While I'm looking through my Rolodex to see who has to go, I always notice some names I haven't been in touch with for a while," she says. "So, while I'm thinking of it, I'll take the time to write a few notes or make some phone calls."

Karen is a first-rate networker, in many ways.

ONE GOOD REASON

There's one good reason why you should help others in your network: If you don't, they won't help you. That's all the reason you need, but there are more:

A WORD TO THE WISE

Susan Larson Williams, vice president for human resources at VF Corporation, says she once met an employee from one of VF Corporation's direct competitors at a conference. She made a point to talk to the person, and they exchanged cards. Shortly after the conference, he called her. She was surprised to hear from him so soon and wondered what he might want. It didn't take long to find out.

The competitor's employee asked for all kinds of information about VF Corporation, much of which was confidential. Susan wasn't about to give this guy any information and was furious that he thought she would. "You really have to watch for people like that who try to take advantage of a networking situation," she warns. "It's a two-way street, but you need to watch out."

- **When you do somebody a favor, they feel like they owe you one.** This position gives you two advantages. It puts you in control of the situation, giving you a psychological advantage, and it makes it easier for you to ask for help when you need it.
- **You'll be perceived as a good person.** Other members of your network will look at you as a real team player if they know you're doing good deeds without even being asked to.
- **It will make you feel good.** Most people really like to help others. Sure, there are days when it seems that everybody wants a piece of you and you wish they'd all just leave you alone, but usually, it's nice to be able to help somebody else.
- **The person you help might take you along for the ride.** Say you help your friend by introducing her to your aunt, the accounting manager. Your friend ends up getting a job in your aunt's department. Now, your friend has a great big addition to her network because she's meeting all kinds of interesting people. She speaks about you in glowing terms to her new networking partners, and suddenly you have new networking partners, too.
- **It's payback for all the times your network has helped you.** Susan Larson Williams keeps that thought in the back of her mind at all times. "If you've gained advantages through networking, and someone helped you along the way," she says, "you need to remember that when somebody calls to network with you."

Networking Notes

- Anyone who thinks that networking is a process designed solely for his or her benefit won't be part of a network for very long.
- Never think that you can't help the other people in your network.
- You can help people in both their professional and personal lives.
- Look for ways to help others in your network *before* they ask for help.
- It's great to be able to help somebody, but be wary of people who would take advantage of you and your connections.
- There are many reasons why you should help other people in your network, but the best reason is because you want to.

CHAPTER | 19

IT'S A SMALL, SMALL WORLD

To most people, a conversation concerning a country such as Benin or Andorra doesn't mean very much. If they've heard of the country at all, it probably was from a small blurb on the international page of the newspaper or was mentioned briefly on the evening news.

Maybe you're content to remain in the dark about what's going on in the rest of the world. After all, many people are concerned only with what directly affects them and their day-to-day lives—get out of bed, read the paper while they eat their Wheaties, go to work, eat a tuna sandwich, come home, eat dinner, take a walk, watch TV, go to bed, then do it all again the next day. They couldn't care less about Benin or Andorra, much less Lesotho or Vanuatu.

If you're curious about this diverse and fascinating world of ours and want to know as much about it and its people as you possibly can, then you have great opportunities ahead of you. With accessible travel and quickly advancing technology that makes it possible to communicate with people in all parts of the world, your possibilities for international networking have a much better chance of becoming reality than they would have even a decade ago.

Just for fun, the next time you have a chance, surf the Internet and see where it takes you. If you don't have Internet access, check your local library. Many have stations for public use, although there may be a small fee and probably a time limit. One advantage of this arrangement is that someone there could show you the basics of Internet use and get you started.

The Internet makes it possible for you to correspond with someone in Zimbabwe, look for a job in Switzerland, learn about employment opportunities in Japan, or check out the economic situation in Malaysia in the same session. Then, you can find out that holiday they're celebrating in France, what kids are learning in schools in Estonia, what the local weather is in Germany, and what crops are growing in China. Pretty amazing, huh?

INTERNATIONAL JOB SEARCH

Did you ever dream of working in a foreign country—working at a ski chalet in Switzerland or learning the ropes from the pastry chef at a French café? What about trying your hand at banking in Bermuda? Engineering in Thailand? Teaching in Kenya? Running a bed and breakfast in Ireland?

If employment in another country sounds like just a dream, dream on! There are dozens of sites on the Internet where you can find out about jobs available abroad. At some sites, you can even post your résumé and apply for the job online. I did my own Internet searches to see what kinds of jobs were available in the international arena.

The Job Search Site

Accessed from the Monster Board (http://www.monster.com), Job Search is a site that allows you to view jobs available across the United States and in many other countries. You select the country and the job area in which you're interested, then request a search.

I searched for a job as an advertising account executive in Germany. Sure enough, one came through. The *European Stars and Stripes* newspaper, based just outside of Frankfurt, was looking for an account executive. The candidate needs at least three years of experience, or a bachelor's degree and one year of experience. The salary was listed at between $28,000 and $35,000, and the total compensation

---

F.Y.I.

Andorra, by the way, is a country half the size of New York City, located in the Pyrenees between Spain and France. Benin is a nation that's slightly smaller than Pennsylvania, located on the Gulf of Guinea in West Africa. Lesotho is a mountainous country in the southern part of Africa, and Vanuatu is sparsely populated island country in the South Pacific.

Now you know!

---

package (including moving expenses and a housing allowance) was $50,000 to 60,000. The application deadline was two weeks from the time I learned the job was available—plenty of time to polish up a résumé and e-mail it off to the contact name, if I had wanted to apply for the job. Those who didn't wish to e-mail a résumé could fax it, and a telephone number also was provided. The site also featured a suggested résumé format, where users could create and send a résumé right away.

I was having so much fun surfing for international jobs that I decided to try another. This time, I searched for a job as a technical writer in France. It's not as romantic a job as a pastry chef in a sidewalk café, but the pay would be better. I found a position that sounded perfect for an aspiring technical writer. It was with a company called Meta4, headquartered in Madrid, Spain. Meta4 has branches in Atlanta, Georgia; São Paolo, Brazil; Mexico City, Mexico; and Paris, France.

I didn't apply for either of these jobs because I'm not qualified—I have no experience in advertising, nor do I have any knowledge of designing and creating technical documentation for software systems. If I had wanted to apply, though, I could have done so immediately—electronically.

Other Site Selections

Many sites offer information about and allow to apply for jobs in other countries. Here are some other sites to browse:

- **Banks of the World** (http://www.wiso.gwdg.de/ifbg/bank-2.html) might be valuable to you if you're interested in a banking career. It includes links to banks in the United States, Asia, Europe, Canada, and other countries; indexes to national and international financial, banking, and currency sites; special discussion groups; and other features.

- **Career Exchange** (http://www.careerexchange.com) is an international career search database with current listings that are updated daily.
- **Jobsite** (http://www.jobsite.co.uk) lists jobs in Europe (Austria, Belgium, Denmark, France, Germany, Italy, Luxembourg, The Netherlands, Norway, Poland, Spain, Sweden, and Switzerland) and the Middle East.
- **Jobz** (http//jobz.ozware.com) posts job opportunities in Australia in areas such as surveying, public relations, printing, sales, government, building, chemistry, oil and gas, hospitality, and travel.
- **Jobware International** (http//www.jobware.de/career.htm) bills itself as "your gateway to multinational employment resources." Jobs are available at companies such as Bayer, Merck, and Hewlett Packard, and locations include Egypt, Luxembourg, and Sweden.
- **Jobmart** (http//www.jobmart.co.uk) posts jobs available in the United Kingdom. Many of the jobs are computer related, but other fields are also included.
- **Malcolm Pacific Hot Jobs** (http://nz.com/webnz/malcolm/hotjobs.html) lists jobs in New Zealand. It also provides information about national regulations concerning immigration, working, and other subjects.
- **World Wide Job Seekers** (http://www.cban.com) posts international jobs in areas such as legal and protective services; science, technical, visual and performing arts; computers and mathematics; accounting and finance; communications; and the health and medical fields. It also has listings for students.

So, if you've always wanted to work abroad, give it a shot. Some Internet sites even have categories for temporary jobs and internships. Using the Internet to find these types of jobs sure beats making expensive international phone calls and mailing letters that could take weeks to arrive.

INTERNATIONAL BUSINESS NEWS

Maybe you're not looking for a job abroad but would like to know more in general about international employment opportunities, economic conditions, and other topics to wow the guests at the next cocktail party you attend. Here are a few sites to get you on your way.

- **The United States Bureau of Labor Statistics** (http://www.bls.gov/) site provides not only reports about U.S. labor markets, hours, wages, productivity, and prices but also information about international labor conditions.
- **CNNfn** (http://www.cnnfn.com/) offers information on U.S. and world markets, currencies, and interest rates.
- **Webgrrl** (http://www/webgrrl.com) is an international site geared toward women who network online and in person. It provides resources for women looking for jobs and for women business owners.
- **The International Herald Tribune** (http://www.iht.com) is the world's daily newspaper—read it online. It provides extensive coverage of many topics of international interest.

OTHER NET RESOURCES

The Internet gives you plenty of opportunities for networking, even if you aren't looking for a job. Remember that a primary function of networking is getting information or knowledge from someone else. Imagine what a vast store of information and knowledge can be obtained via the Internet.

In a 1994 interview with National Public Radio, David Farber, professor of telecommunications at the University of Pennsylvania in Philadelphia, estimated that 20 million were using the Internet internationally. No doubt, the number has increased dramatically since then. Interestingly, he said the majority of people using the Internet for international purposes were not people in the computer business or those related to colleges and universities, as had been the case previously. They were just folks cruising around in cyberspace, looking to see what they'd find. He also noted that computers have replaced ham radios as the means of choice for relaying messages back and forth during times of disaster.

Booking a Flight or a Hotel Room

When you decide to travel, you can use the Internet to make airline and hotel reservations and never end up waiting on hold while the reservations person helps someone else. A few sites to get you started are the following:

- **The HOTTEST Airfares on Earth** (http://www.etn.nl/hotfares.html)
- **European Travel Network** (http://www.etn.nl/index.html)

- **Air Traveler's Handbook Home Page** (http://www.cs.cmu.edu/afs/cs/user/mkant/Public/Travel/airfare.html)

Making Strangers Less Strange

Perhaps the most fascinating aspect of the Internet is that it has the ability to connect people. Sure, we can get tons of information about international business and travel. We can find the best international air fares and find a great hotel in Istanbul. Most amazingly, we can meet people from all over the world and learn about their cultures, thoughts, and lives.

I certainly don't mean to give the impression that people in every hamlet and village are sitting at their computers, waiting to chat via the Internet to network with a curious American. Still, a look at some Web sites reveals that many countries are well represented in cyberspace.

Browsing at one Web site, I found more than 200 people logged on in about 30 different discussion groups, representing countries including Brazil, the United Kingdom, Canada, China, Denmark, Finland, Germany, Greece, India, Ireland, Israel, Italy, Japan, Malaysia, Mexico, South Africa, Spain, and Sweden.

At another site, I chatted with a Japanese man who lives in Osaka, on the west coast of Japan. In the 10 minutes we were online together, I learned he had studied for four years in the United States. Because of this he had excellent English skills and a real interest in communicating with Americans. He told me a little about his family in Japan, his job, and his plans for the future.

Internet networking can't replace face-to-face networking, because you can't shake hands or smile in cyberspace. Nor should it. But it's an amazing feeling to sit at your computer at 9:30 on a Monday morning and know you're hooked up with someone half-way around the world.

BE CAREFUL!

If you've never delved extensively into the Internet, be prepared to experience how much time it takes. Even if you intend to spend only a few minutes online, your session usually ends up being much longer. It's too easy to check out "just a couple more links."

Remember that it's dangerous to let your online time infringe on what you need to do in real time.

Some Sites to Check Out (When You Have Time)

Here are some chat sites designed to put you in touch with people from other countries.

- **Web of Culture** (http://www.worldculture.com) topics include cross-cultural exchanges, international music and politics, and more.
- At **PlaySite** (http://www.playsite.com), you can hook up with someone from China and play checkers online. It gives a whole new meaning to Chinese checkers!
- The **Virtual Irish Pub** (http://www.visunet.ie/vip/welcome.html) invites you to grab a brew and have a little chat. Who knows who you'll meet?
- **Lonely Planet Online** (http://lonelyplanet.com) gives you a chance to ask a lot of questions to world travelers before you book a trip. Online tours of different places are offered, and lots of tips and advice are offered.
- At the **Café de Paris** (http://paris-anglo.com/cafe), you can chat with Parisians, in French or in English, from your own home.
- **Kid's Space Connection** (http://www.ks-connection.com) gives kids their own place to hook up with and learn about kids from different countries and cultures. They also can share their favorites stories and art.
- **Global Study Chat** (http://www.globalstudy.com/cgi-bin/chatpro.cgi/) is a place to chat with people of all different nationalities who are studying English in the United States, Canada, Great Britain, Ireland, Australia, and New Zealand.

REMEMBER YOUR MANNERS

When you chat on the Internet, there's a code of conduct called "netiquette" that must be followed.

Netiquette varies from discussion group to discussion group and from chat room to chat room, so it's a good idea to hang around a site first until you get the feel of what's expected. However, some general rules apply most anywhere online:

- **Express yourself clearly and concisely.** Watch your spelling and grammar, and try to make sure that what you're typing will make sense to the person reading it.

- **Respect the people you're chatting with.** It's fine to disagree with someone, but it is unacceptable to start name-calling online. Address the topic of discussion—don't verbally attack the person with whom you disagree.
- **Avoid offensive language!** Many segments of the population—including children—are included in online discussions. Vulgar or hateful language serves no purpose in these discussion groups.
- **Respond only if you're informed about the topic.** Strut your stuff when it's warranted, but don't post incorrect information just so you have something to say.
- **Don't type in ALL CAPITAL LETTERS.** It's considered yelling—bad manners!—is hard to read, and can be distracting.
- **If you ask a lot of personal questions, offer some information about yourself.** If you are not prepared to tell others about yourself, you shouldn't expect them to tell you.
- **Check the rules before you jump online.** Different Internet service providers have established different regulations regarding discussion groups and chat rooms. Netiquette, however, is pretty much the same all over the Internet.

FIND OLD FRIENDS

Remember the exchange student from New Zealand who was in your 10th grade class? You used to joke with her all the time in math class. Do you ever wonder where she is now?

What about those British camp counselors at the camp where you worked summers during college? Remember all the good times you had together? Ever wonder how they're doing?

It might be a challenge, but it would be well worth it as far as your network is concerned to reestablish contact with some long-lost foreign friends. There are ways to do Internet searches to locate someone, but you do need some information. Flip through some of your old address books to find the last address you had for that person. It might be 10 years old, but it could be your friend's parents' address. If they still live there, they could help put you in touch.

Think about other people who were friends with the person you want to locate. Maybe some of those people kept in touch. If you can figure out how to contact them, you might be able to reestablish contact with your foreign friend.

Reestablishing communication with friends in other countries may seem like a daunting task, but our world really is getting smaller all the time. New Zealand is hardly inaccessible. Who knows when you might someday schedule a trip to Auckland, and wouldn't it be nice to be able to catch up with an old friend when you're there?

International Networking Is Getting Easier and Easier

I remember clearly, 20 years ago, standing in a red phone box somewhere in rural England, trying to call home to Pennsylvania. It took a long time, a pocketful of coins, and a lot of patience to finally get a connection that was about as clear as talking with a mouthful of peanut butter.

These days, we have phone service that makes it nearly impossible to tell whether we're calling from across town or half-way around the world. With those same phone lines, we can fax documents, e-mail messages, and chat on the Internet in real time. We also can reserve our flights and accommodations online when we decide to travel.

Networking internationally is getting easier all the time, and those who overlook it are missing out on some exciting and rewarding connections.

Networking Notes

- Possibilities for international networking increase dramatically with the use of the Internet.
- The Internet can be especially useful if you're looking for a job overseas.
- International business news is accessible 24 hours a day on the Internet.
- The Internet allows you to book international travel on your own.
- There's a whole world of people waiting to meet you online.
- Remember your manners when you're chatting on the Internet.

CHAPTER | 20

NETWORKING FOR LIFE

I hope you feel that you know a lot more about networking since you first picked up this book. You have learned a lot:

- How to navigate the job market, launch the Great Job Hunt, and do the best you possibly can when it comes to informational interviews, résumés, job interviews, and building your network from the ground up
- What "network" and "networking" mean, how networks work, and what networks do
- Which tools you'll need to succeed in networking, how to identify the people who should be included in your network, and how to determine what each person has to offer
- How to convince somebody to network with you, how and where to recognize a potential addition to your network, and how to follow up after you establish a contact

- Where to find valuable information and how to recognize situations, on the job and off, in which your network will be valuable
- That it's at least as important to *give* help when you can, in both personal and professional situations, and to help out before you're asked
- That international networking is becoming increasingly common and easier than ever before, thanks to expanding technology

In addition to the basics of networking, I hope I conveyed to you the *spirit* of networking. This spirit embodies cooperation, mutual benefit, concern for the other people, common sense, enthusiasm, and caring. If you learn anything from this book, I want it to be this understanding about the networking process. Networking can work only when it's a mutual effort, and from that effort, networkers reap mutual rewards.

A strong network will last you a lifetime. You will see other members of your network through the good and bad times in life, and they'll do the same for you. You'll use your network during your entire career and then to help your children and grandchildren with their careers. You'll use it for not only business but also for social and personal reasons. You'll make many friends through your network, and learn that's the best reason to network in the first place. Your network will remain a source of strength and joy, but you have to know how to make it survive—and stay young.

WHY WE START, AND WHERE WE FINISH

Although nearly everyone networks throughout their entire lives, most people don't begin thinking about it until they start looking for a job. Only then does networking becomes a focused, intensive effort.

You go through all the steps: identifying a job you want, making the connections, doing the interviews and the follow-ups, and whatever else it takes to get that job. Then, you have a job as well as a network. The network continues to grow while you work. You add coworkers, employers, the competition, suppliers, salespeople, lawyers, and accountants—whoever you happen to meet along the way.

When you see your network at work and note how it comes through for you, you realize the enormity of the networking concept. You come to fully understand how much you depend on your network and how the other members in it depend on you. You begin to follow up more earnestly on contacts and find out a little bit more about the people whose names are in your card file already. You start meeting for lunch or maybe for dinner with your significant others.

If a promotion comes your way, your network congratulates you. If downsizing leaves you jobless, your network empathizes with you, supports you, and stands behind you while you plunge back into the market to find another job.

Sure, some members of your network will be more active and more involved than others, but if one person can't be relied on to come through in a pinch, there's a weak spot in your network that will weaken the entire structure.

Like a marriage or a friendship, networking requires commitment and hard work. If all parties are not willing to work at making the relationship successful, it won't be. It grows stronger and stronger over the years in a quiet, solid sort of way. You learn to trust it completely and to respect and treasure the loyalty that comes from within it.

STANDING THE TEST OF TIME

I know a group of five women, all in their early 40s, who have been friends since junior high school. Two of them have been friends since first grade. Three of them went to the same church and have known each other since they were kids. Their group was fully formed when they were all about 15 years old.

Some of these women have moved away, but even the ones that live near each other don't get together very often. Jobs, homes, husbands, kids, and other responsibilities fill up days, nights, and weekends.

As among almost any friends, the dynamics of the group are continually changing. One person's feelings get hurt when another comes to town and doesn't get in touch. Another feels left out because she's not invited to lunch with two others. Something happens that bonds two or three of the women even more closely together than usual.

This extremely close network doesn't work perfectly, but it has worked continuously for more than 25 years. It's impossible to know how many instances of networking have occurred among these women, but it's certainly in the thousands. They've supported each other through junior high school dances and high school proms, thwarted romances and broken hearts, college final exams, graduations, and first jobs. Marriages, births, deaths, and turning 40 have all been made more joyous or easier to bear because of each other.

The single most important ingredient of this network, according to its members, is trust. Each one trusts the others to be there whenever she needs it. That's not to say that they never disagree about how something should be handled or criticize how someone responded to a situation. It doesn't mean that each woman will physically be there each time a member of the group needs help or support. However, there's implicit trust among these women that, if one member has a need, the others will do everything they can to support her. There are no weak links in this network.

Although this informal networking group has its share of egos and pettiness, it embodies the spirit of networking as well as any group I've ever seen. Can you imagine the rewards of belonging to such a group?

Any one of these women, or anyone else who's a member of a strong network, will tell you that the rewards of networking don't come for free. The network must be kept strong and in working order. If the network isn't maintained, it will fall apart, and nobody will benefit from it.

Rest assured that the rewards and satisfaction of networking are well worth the effort of keeping it strong and healthy. So, you ask, how do you keep a network going? What does it take?

BACK WHERE YOU STARTED

Remember the qualities you needed to get your network started? Among them were perseverance, enthusiasm, honesty, a willingness to help, sincerity, organization, and a genuine desire to create a successful network. Those same qualities are necessary to keep a network strong and operational.

Whether your network is for business or personal use, you have to work to keep in touch with the other members. Even the five women mentioned above have to make a collective effort to keep in touch by phone, notes, e-mails, and occasional visits. It's not always easy, but the results are worth it.

Keeping in Touch

There are dozens of ways to keep in touch with members of your network. Most of them don't require any great expense, too much time, or inordinate amount of effort.

Sending a Card

I used to think that sending birthday cards to business associates or clients was a contrived, artificial method of networking. Then, after I had started working on this book, I got a birthday postcard from my chiropractor's office that said, "You're one in a million." On the other side was, "And you're number one with us! Have a happy, healthy birthday!"

The card arrived a week before my birthday, and guess what? I fell for it—hook, line, and sinker. I was as pleased as punch with this card. It wasn't hand addressed; it wasn't even signed! It was just a simple postcard, with the name of the practice in the top corner of the back side. (My chiropractor later told me, rather proudly, that his new computer program allows them to run a set of labels each month, which they stick on ready-printed cards.) Despite all the things it wasn't, that card was is an effective means of creating good will. Because every patient gets one, it's also a great way of keeping in touch with patients who come to the office only a couple of times of year.

"I used to send out postcards reminding patients that they should call for an appointment for a checkup," the owner of the practice explains, "but that seemed like I was bugging them. I think the birthday cards achieve pretty much the same thing, because they remind patients that we're here. I always get calls from patients who say they just got the birthday card and they want to make an appointment."

Mortgage broker Chris Flynn swears by birthday cards as an effective method of networking. He makes a point of learning his clients' birthdays so he can be sure to send a card, and he gets a lot of positive feedback—and some business, too—as a result of birthday cards. "The truth is that most adults don't get many birthday cards," he says. "They really appreciate it when somebody remembers them."

Anniversary and holiday cards also are good methods of keeping in touch. Remember that some people are especially enthusiastic about certain holidays. If you know someone who, for some reason, is wild about Independence Day, go out of your way to find a card to send him. A Fourth of July card will be remembered long after that big batch of Christmas cards is forgotten.

Some experts recommend sending holiday cards at Thanksgiving instead of Christmas or Hanukkah. A Thanksgiving Day card will stand out in a crowd and probably will be saved or displayed along with the other holiday cards.

Always send a card or note to members of your network who have been promoted, changed jobs, become parents, lost family members, or experienced any other major life events. Remember that cards aren't just for businesspeople. Personal cards are appreciated and can be sent for any occasion—or just to say hello.

F.Y.I.

There are many places to find greeting cards suitable for business. You can even contact these two online:

- **Animal Grams Cards for Businesses** (http://www.greetings-gifts.com): Call 914-424-3149 or fax to 914-424-4239.
- **Data Tron's Quality Business Printing** (http://www.datatron.net/dthead.htm): Call 305-273-1151.

Also, check your local office supply store to see what they have available.

Drop By When You're in the Neighborhood

One of the biggest problems among those women I talked about earlier was when one woman and her family visited a tourist site about 30 miles from the home of another. The woman and her family spent a day there and then, without even calling her friend who lived nearby, turned around and went back to the home of the relatives with whom they were staying. These women hadn't seen each other for more than a year, but the visitor didn't take the time to make a contact.

Talk about hurt feelings!

At the very least, the woman visiting the tourist site should have called her friend. She could have explained that time was very short or whatever and they wouldn't have time to visit. Perhaps the other woman would have offered to drive to the tourist site and meet her friend for lunch. Regardless, the effort would have been made and the strife avoided.

Keep Your Network Informed

Keep the members of your network informed of what you've been doing. Have you moved recently or taken a great trip? Send postcards from your new address or your vacation destination—Stockholm, Milan, or Disney World.

Let people know what's going on in your life: a new baby, a new pet, or a new job. Of course, you don't have to sit down and write 80 notes every time something of significance happens to you! Target the people in your network to whom you think the news most directly applies or those who will be most interested.

Exchange E-mail Addresses

The Internet represents many things to many people, but one thing for sure is that it's a great way to keep in touch. E-mail has brought many people back in touch and makes it easy for those who already were in touch to stay that way.

With e-mail, you can quickly dash off a note to your best friend in Florida, your sister in Kansas City, or your boss in his office. It's a highly efficient, inexpensive, and convenient way of keeping in touch and a wonderful tool for networking. Get as many e-mail addresses as you can, and keep a record of them. More and more people are including e-mail addresses on their personal stationery and business cards, so you will collect them in no time.

Any News Is Good News

When you read something that's especially interesting, clip it and send it to someone in your network. It doesn't have to be earth-shattering news, just something that you have in common with that person or that you know that person will like.

If when you read an article about singer Billy Joel, for example, you immediately think of your friend who goes to his every concert, then send it to your friend. It's a perfect opportunity to check in and say hello. If an article in this month's issue of your favorite magazine reminds you of a conversation about the benefits of organic produce that you had with your boss' wife last week, then send her a copy. She will appreciate that you remembered that conversation, and you just might make some points with your boss, too.

It doesn't matter what it is, as long as it's of interest to someone in your network. Clipping and sending an article is a small but a much appreciated gesture. It's a great way to stay in touch.

Do Something Extra-Nice

Most people get a gift or two on their birthdays and presents at Christmas or Hanukkah. Graduations, Mother's Day, and Father's Day also can be cause to buy and deliver flowers or some other token of affection, appreciation, or congratulations.

Why wait for a holiday or special occasion? If you see something that somebody you know will just love and you're in a position to buy it, go ahead and get it. Looking at that gift will make the person who receives it think of you and remember your kindness.

Thoughtfulness has other forms, too. How many people do you know that would really appreciate it if you stopped by or called unexpectedly, just to say hello? It doesn't take a lot of time, or money, or effort to make someone feel good or special, but such gestures go a long way toward cementing a relationship and making that person's day a little bit brighter.

Think about ways you can express, "I'm thinking of you," "I appreciate you," or "I'm glad to know you." Thoughtful gestures are nice anytime, but they're especially nice when they're unexpected.

WHAT IF YOU OUTLIVE YOUR NETWORK?

A good network will be a network for life, but what happens if you outlive your network? You build another!

My grandmother, Ethel Klaus, celebrated her 100th birthday on August 17, 1998. Imagine waking up one morning and knowing you've lived for an entire century! As anyone who has lived as long, she has experienced a lot of joy and a lot of sorrow.

Ethel never called her network a network; those people were just people she knew—neighbors and club members, relatives she didn't see very often, and others she saw every day. Some she loved, some she did business with. Still, these people were her support, her help, and the ones she helped.

A special part of Ethel's network was a group of elderly people who had summer homes in a small community in southeastern Pennsylvania. It was a quiet rural spot where people would come from Philadelphia and other towns to spend the summers in pleasant cottages surrounded by tall oak and pine trees. Summer evenings were spent sitting on the wide front porches or in screened-in rooms, playing cards, drinking tall glasses of iced tea, and talking late into the night. It was a special group of friends who had shared their summers for many years.

Time passed, and some of the members of the group became ill. One by one, death took these integral members of Ethel's network. Her husband died, her friends died, and two of her five children died.

At some point, Ethel and her family decided it was time for a change. In her mid 90s, Ethel could no longer maintain her home or drive her car. Cooking was too much of a chore, and her family worried about her. So, she moved into a small residential home in Pottstown, Pennsylvania, and set about rebuilding her network. There, she made a new best friend, with whom she spends many hours of each day. She got to know all the people who work at the home and is a favorite among the other residents. The oldest person there, she is one of the most lively and outgoing.

At age 100, Ethel's new network is strong. Other than the core of her network—her family—it contains few of the same members as 25 years ago. She outlived practically her entire network, so she built a new one. It continues to enrich her life and make her happy for the 100 years she's had.

Not all of us will live to be 100, but no matter how long we spend on this earth, one thing is for sure. Like it did for my grandmother, a strong network of supportive, caring people will enhance the joys we'll find in life and will make the sorrows easier to bear.

Networking Notes

- A strong network will serve you, and you it, for your entire life.
- If maintained properly, your network will make your joys more joyful and your sorrows less bleak.
- Maintaining a good network requires effort, but the rewards are well worth it.
- Think of ways to keep in touch with other people in your network. Send cards, notes, interesting articles, and e-mail messages.
- Unexpected, thoughtful gestures go a long way toward cementing relationships and keeping your network strong.
- If you outlive your network, you'll have to build another.

APPENDIX

ADDITIONAL RESOURCES

Now that you've mastered the basics of networking, you might want to get some different perspectives and learn even more about the topic. Check out some of these books, which offer tips and advice. If you have access to the Internet, refer back to the Web sites listed throughout this book.

Charland, William. *The Complete Idiot's Guide to Changing Careers.* New York: Alpha Books/Macmillan, 1998.

Fein, Richard. *First Job: A New Grad's Guide to Launching Your Business Career.* New York: John Wiley & Sons, Inc., 1992.

Grappo, Gary Joseph. *The Top 10 Career Strategies for the Year 2000 and Beyond.* New York: Berkley Books, 1997.

Heenehan, Meg. *Job Notes: Networking.* New York: Random House, Inc., 1997.

Hewitt, Linda. *Networking for the Career-Minded Student.* Atlanta, GA: Lenox Publishing Co., 1995.

Hyatt, Carole. *Shifting Careers: How to Master Career Change and Find the Right Work for You.* New York: Simon and Schuster, 1990.

Krannich, Dr. Ronald L. *Careering and Re-Careering for the 90s* (3rd ed.). Las Cruces, NM: Impact Publications, Inc., 1993.

Mackay, Harvey. *Dig Your Well Before You're Thirsty.* New York: Doubleday, 1997.

McManus, Judith A. *Effective Business Speaking: The Basics Made Easy.* New York: LearningExpress, 1998.

Networking, The Wall Street Journal National Business Employment Weekly. New York: John Wiley & Sons, Inc., 1994.

Quamstrom, Melody Shart. *Getting On Top.* New York: Price Stern Sloan, Inc., 1988.

Sheldon, Betsy, and Joyce Hadley. *The Smart Woman's Guide to Networking.* Franklin Lakes, NJ: The Career Press, Inc., 1995.

Sonnenblick, Carol, Michaele Basciano, and Kim Crabbe. *Job Hunting Made Easy.* New York: LearningExpress, 1997.

Tulgan, Bruce. *Work This Way.* New York: Hyperion, 1998.